GW01607338

HIGHLIGHTS GERMANY

THE 50 MOST BEAUTIFUL PLACES TO SEE

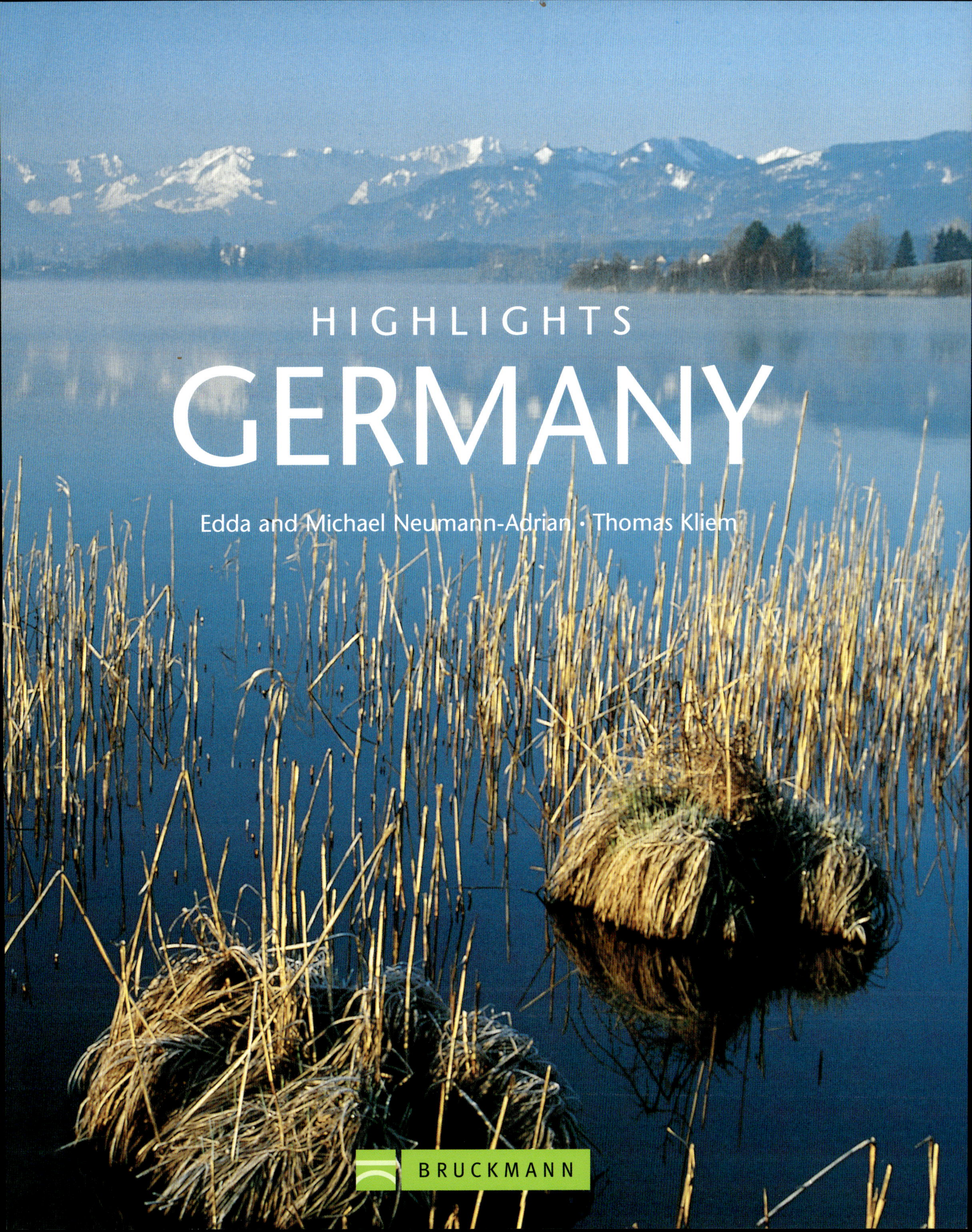

HIGHLIGHTS

GERMANY

Edda and Michael Neumann-Adrian · Thomas Kliem

BRUCKMANN

Above: a seaside resort for over one hundred years: Sellin, plus pier, on the Mönchgut peninsula on the island of Rügen.
Centre: The North goes for colour: the Blue House in Zingst
Below: A jewel in the green heart of Germany: Bamberg with the Concordia Garden Palace on the River Regnitz

Table of Contents

Above: Fairy-tale castle in the Bavarian Alps: Castle Schachen features an unusual oriental interior.
Centre: Alpine summers at their best: the Zugspitze looks down onto flowering meadows.
Below: The Karwendel Massif near Mittenwald reflected in quiet lake waters.

North Sea
Baltic Sea
Highlights
0
50 km
N
Westerland
SYLT
Niebüll
NORTH FRISIAN ISLANDS
Flensburg
Husum
Schleswig
Kiel
Heide
HELGOLAND
Eutin
Neumünster
Itzehohe
Brunsbüttel
Lübeck
Puttgarden
FEHMARN
RÜGEN
Jasmund National Park
Saßnitz
Western Pommerania's Bodden Landscape
Stralsund
Greifswald
USEDOM
Anklam
Rostock
Güstrow
Wismar
EAST FRISIAN ISLANDS
SPIEKEROOG
Cuxhaven
Norden
Aurich
Jever
Wilhelms-haven
Emden
Leer
Eastern Friesland
Oldenburg
Delmenhorst
Bremer-haven
Stade
Elbe
Weser
Hamburg
Worpswede
Bremen
Ratze-burg
Schwerin
Lauenburg
Ludwigslust
Neubrandenburg
Mecklenburg Lake Plateau
Müritz
Neustrelitz
Prenzlau
Mirow
Rheinsberg
Gransee
Schwedt
Lüneburg
Luneburg Heath
Soltau
Verden
Uelzen
Wittenberge
Neuruppin
Havelberg
Havel
Salzwedel
Altmark
Stendal
Ems
Quaken-brück
Meppen
Nienburg
Celle
Berlin
Nauen
Branden-burg
Potsdam
Fürstenwalde
Frankfurt/O.
Spre
Lehrte
Wolfsburg
Aller
Rheine
Osna-brück
Minden
Hannover
Hameln
Braunschweig
Königslutter
Elm
Magdeburg
Hildes-heim
Salzgitter
Münster
Münsterland
Gütersloh
Bielefeld
Bad Harzburg
Goslar
Quedlinburg
Lutherstadt Wittenberg
Spree Forest Biosphere Reserve
Xanten
Reckling-hausen
Weserberg-land
Holzminden
Harz
Thale
Bernburg
Dessau
Cottbus
Lausitzer
Hamm
Paderborn
Göttingen
Finsterwalde
Duisburg
Bochum
Essen
Dortmund
Nord-hausen
Lutherstadt Eisleben
Halle
Torgau
Hoyerswerda
Krefeld
Sauerland
Münden
Heiligenstadt
Merseburg
Saale
Leipzig
Düsseldorf
Wuppertal
Kassel
Mühlhausen
Sonders-hausen
Naumburg
Bautzen
Görlitz
Meißen
Dresden
Upper Lusatia
Leverkusen
Fulda
Wartburg
Gotha
Erfurt
Weimar
Saxon Switzerland
Zittau
Cologne
Siegen
Bad Hersfeld
Eisenach
Dornburg
Jena
Chemnitz
Aachen
Bonn
Rhine
Marburg
Thuringian Forest
Gera
Zwickau
Erzgebirge
Westerwald
Lahn
Rhön
Saalfeld
Annaberg-Buchholz
Neuwied
Wetzlar
Gießen
Fulda
Meiningen
Eifel
Koblenz
Bad Nauheim
Plauen
Vogt-land
Burg Eltz
Taunus
Coburg
Hof
Cochem
Rheingau
Frankfurt
Bad Kissingen
Seßlach
Franconian Forest
Winkel
Wiesbaden
Schweinfurt
Mainz
Aschaffenburg
Bingen
Darm-stadt
Bayreuth
Markt-redwitz
Bohemian Forests
Moselle
Main
Wurzburg
Bamberg
Trier
Idar-Oberstein
Worms
Bens-heim
Tauber-bischofsheim
Kitzingen
Weiden
Franconian Alb
Ludwigshafen
Erlangen
Saar-brücken
Kaisers-lautern
Tauber
Fürth
Nuremberg
Amberg
Speyer
Heidelberg
Rothenburg ob der Tauber
Ansbach
Schwabach
Cham
Pirmasens
Heilbronn
Gr. Arber
Karlsruhe
Schwäbisch-Hall
Dinkelsbühl
Regens-burg
Zwiesel
Bavarian Forest
Rastatt
Pforzheim
Neckar
Aalen
Nördlingen
Eichstätt
Straubing
Baden-Baden
Stuttgart
Donau-wörth
Ingolstadt
Deggendorf
Tübingen
Geislingen
Alps
Danube
Isar
Passau
Offenburg
Landshut
Reutlingen
Swabian
Freising
Ulm
Neu-Ulm
Mühldorf
Black Forest
Augsburg
Dachau
Breisgau
Biberach
Landsberg
Munich
Inn
Frei-burg
Tuttlingen
Memmingen
Starnberg
Rosen-heim
Chiem-see
Traunstein
Singen
MAINAU
Ravensburg
Kaufbeuren
Chiemgau
Freilassing
Schaffhausen
Meersburg
Kempten
Wies
Staffelsee
Lörrach
Constance
Allgäu
Füssen
Oberammergau
Berchtesgaden
Lake Constance
Lindau
Neuschwan-stein
Garmisch-Partenkirchen
Watzmann
Berchtesgaden National Park
Zugspitze
Alps

Above: Mighty walls overlooking Riesling vineyards: Castle Johannisberg in the Rheingau region. Centre: Germany's second largest body of water: Lake Müritz in southern Pomerania. Below: Rheinsberg Castle, made famous by the Prussian King Frederick II and Kurt Tucholsky. Opposite: Moated castle of Raesfeld in the Münster region.

Germany at its most Beautiful

Our world has much to offer in the way of spectacular sights: places of great natural beauty and landmarks of cultural significance. From the pyramids to the Taj Mahal, the Eiffel Tower, the palaces built by Peter the Great and the gardens of the Alhambra – there's so much to see. We wish every one of you the chance to visit your own personal favourites and are delighted to present you with our own selection of sights in Germany, a country rich in natural diversity, beautiful cities and unsurpassed architecture.

The destinations presented in this book are relatively easy to reach: situated in the heart of Europe, Germany is served by a dense network of road, rail and air traffic connections. German reunification in 1989 added a whole series of additional sights to an already impressive register, with destinations such as the Erzgebirge and the Baltic Sea, which were previously inaccessible to all but the local inhabitants, suddenly becoming available to a wide and appreciative travelling public.

How did we go about identifying the fifty most beautiful places in Germany – cultural sites and natural landscapes, castles and palaces, old towns and churches, mountains, rivers and lakes? There were three criteria to be observed:

The first of these was doubtless an appreciation of "beauty". Although "most beautiful" tends to be a subjective classification, there will always be a certain consensus on sites that are worth seeing. So far, over 50 million people have deemed Neuschwanstein Palace such a place. Soon, it may be over 100 million.

Our choices also concentrated on places and landscapes which are not spoiled by excessive traffic, construction sins or hordes of tourists: places which remain easy to enjoy and encourage relaxation.

And thirdly: it would have been easy to extend the list to include one hundred, maybe even two hundred sites. Despite the ravages of World War II, Germany is still rich in old or reconstructed city centres. In the face of large-scale urbanisation, it has maintained a wealth of natural beauty in its landscapes.

Time travel through the centuries to acquaint oneself with the variety of landscapes between the oceans and mountains that encircle Germany is a task of many years. The beaches and waters of Germany's North and Baltic Sea coastlines, together with the Bavarian Alps and Alpine foothills, are the

Germany is famous for its lakes and rivers. Above: Grosser Plöner See near Bosau. Centre: Excursion boats being punted through the quiet waters of the Spree Forest. Below: The gables and towers on the harbour of Lindau on Lake Constance. Above right: The village of Königssee and the mountains beyond.

country's most popular holiday destinations, but there's an abundance of beauty to be found in the centre as well. Our journeys took us up and down rivers – and not just the famous ones such as the Rhine and the Elbe but smaller ones too, like the Tauber and the Saale. This latter river, at least, is still largely unknown in western and southern Germany – despite the wonderful verses penned by Germany's national poet, Johann Wolfgang von Goethe (1749–1832), on Dornburg's castles. It's amazing to note how little the landscape between Dornburg and Jena has changed since his lifetime.

The same applies to the Altmark region. Where's that? Not all that many former West Germans know either. The answer would be: around the little towns of Stendal, Tangermünde and Havelberg on the Elbe and Havel rivers, which have long since discarded their dowdy GDR mantle in favour of fresher colours and are filled with vibrant culture enlivening their old city centres.

You'll find many such places in this book: small and medium-sized towns such as Freiburg and Heidelberg, Ulm and Goslar, Bamberg in Franconia and the tiny town of Sesslach. Compare them to the cities of Mecklenburg-Western Pomerania, Saxony-Anhalt or Thuringia – to towns such as Stralsund, Quedlinburg or Eisenach – and you'll be surprised to note that years of neglect during the GDR had its advantages. Some historic buildings were simply forgotten. Other "feudal" constructions were torn down to make way for less ideologically suspect constructions. But many towns in the GDR lacked the funds to replace old town centres with department stores and administrative centres, or build apartment blocks between the spires of Romanesque and Gothic cathedrals (although Jena was saddled with its skyscraper). When the wall came down in 1989, it was high time to act – but it was not too late, and many cities in eastern Germany are better off than their counterparts in the west, where the post-war building boom did more to destroy historic structures than Hitler.

World Heritage sites, national parks and citizens' action groups

The number of German cathedrals, castles and old town centres on the UNESCO World Heritage List continues to grow. Along with France and Italy, Germany is now one of the countries with the greatest density of culturally significant sites (for a current overview, check www.worldheritagesite.org). This

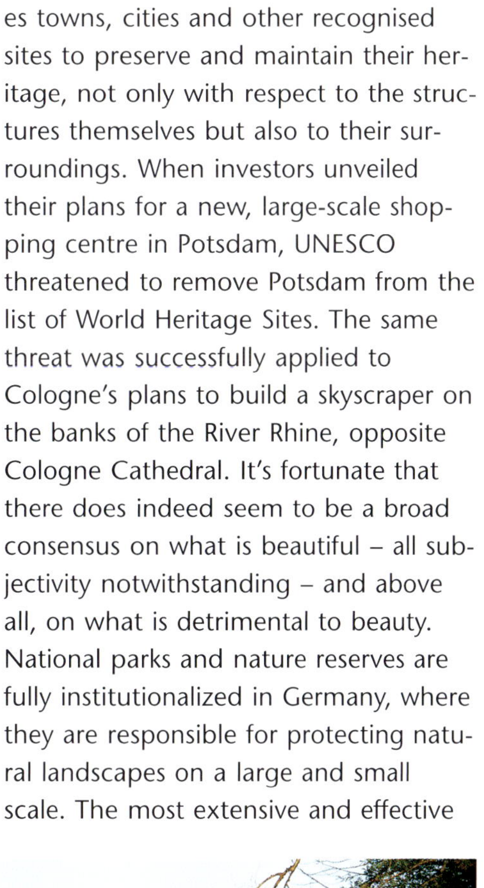

list is not just a tourist magnet. It obliges towns, cities and other recognised sites to preserve and maintain their heritage, not only with respect to the structures themselves but also to their surroundings. When investors unveiled their plans for a new, large-scale shopping centre in Potsdam, UNESCO threatened to remove Potsdam from the list of World Heritage Sites. The same threat was successfully applied to Cologne's plans to build a skyscraper on the banks of the River Rhine, opposite Cologne Cathedral. It's fortunate that there does indeed seem to be a broad consensus on what is beautiful – all subjectivity notwithstanding – and above all, on what is detrimental to beauty. National parks and nature reserves are fully institutionalized in Germany, where they are responsible for protecting natural landscapes on a large and small scale. The most extensive and effective

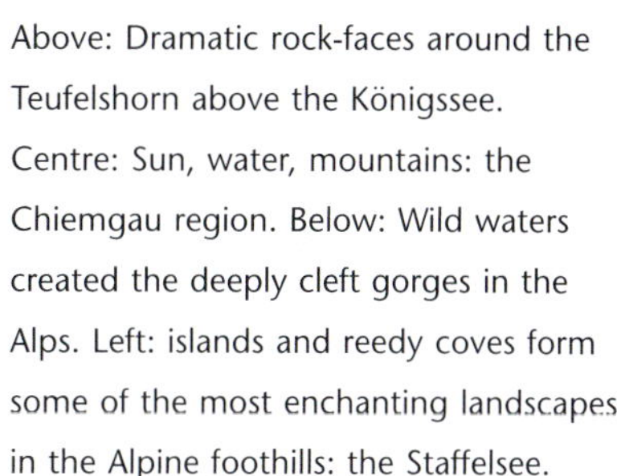

Above: Dramatic rock-faces around the Teufelshorn above the Königssee. Centre: Sun, water, mountains: the Chiemgau region. Below: Wild waters created the deeply cleft gorges in the Alps. Left: islands and reedy coves form some of the most enchanting landscapes in the Alpine foothills: the Staffelsee.

Above: A splendid pavilion forms the centrepiece of Dresden's Zwinger Museum. Centre: Violinmakers in Mittenwald. Below: Transparent tent roofs span Munich's Olympic Stadium. Right: These lime trees near Bad Doberan now form part of Germany's network of tree-lined roads known as the Alleenstrasse.

plans for the protection of the natural environment were put into place at the end of the GDR era: Honecker's regime was not known for ecological prudence, but conservationists had been hard at work drawing up plans for national parks and when the Wall came down, they used the unification treaty as an opportunity to implement them. Today, large areas of land from the island of Rügen to Saxon Switzerland form part of these parks: it's nothing short of miraculous. The unification treaty confirmed these projects and Germany's overall nature protection record improved considerably. Most of today's national park regions are undoubtedly some of the finest landscapes in the country.

There are many examples of citizens' action groups playing a decisive role in the preservation or reconstruction of ancient landmarks. It was the people of Dresden, for example, who began collecting money for the reconstruction of the completely destroyed Frauenkirche (Church of Our Lady), and persevered with the project, raising millions of euros before it was completed. The church was re-consecrated in 2005 and the architectural heart of Dresden – from the terraces down by the River Elbe to the world-famous museums, from the old market to the opera house – is enjoying a new lease of life. One of the most courageous, imaginative and elegant constructions built in the second half of the 20th century – Munich's Olympic Stadium – was threatened with modification, possibly even demolition. As a long-time home to the German soccer team Bayern Munich it almost became obsolete when it was decided that a new stadium was needed: something more modern, more contemporary, the kind of witches' cauldron in which fans can really let rip. The architects of the original stadium, Günther Behnisch and Frei Otto, could have asserted their copyright and might have agreed to a modification but so many locals protested against the planned alterations to their beloved Olympic Park that the city relented: the old stadium, with its wonderfully translucent roof, was placed under a preservation order and Bayern Munich football team joined forces with the other major Munich soccer team, the 1860 Lions, and built a new stadium on the northern outskirts of the city: the Allianz Arena, with its illuminated outer skin.

Beauty is not a static quality. It needs to be constantly re-discovered and defended. We hope you will enjoy joining us on this mission, with trips to 50 widely differing destinations, helping where you can to preserve the manifold beauty of Germany's towns and landscapes.

And where will you stay?

Travelling is most enjoyable when there is somewhere truly pleasant to relax at the end of the day. We have looked around for hotels and inns that are famous for their hospitality and characterised by their beautiful location. Our proposals vary in price: one for each destination. If you'd like to check out alternatives, just contact the tourist bureaus whose addresses we've also provided along with corresponding websites.

Michael and Edda Neumann

Northern Germany goes for colour: Above: The blue barn on Hiddensee. Center: Blaues Haus (Blue House) in the popular village of Zingst/Darss. Below: The picturesque Heiliggeist Monastery in Stralsund. Right: a seaside resort for over one hundred years: Sellin, plus pier, on the Mönchgut peninsula on the island of Rügen.

Germany's North

Center: At the "elbow" in the north of the long, narrow island. Below: Beach in front of the Red Cliffs near Kampen, a popular meeting place for the rich and beautiful. Right: Lighthouse near the village of List. Sea-lovers come in their thousands each year and yet Sylt still has peace and its very own special atmosphere to offer.

1 Sylt – North Sea Jewel

A German dream

"Sea. Passion. Life" is the motto on recent brochures promoting the attractions of Sylt: a holiday here is more than just a holiday. It is elemental, existential. It's over 150 years since the islanders founded the resort of Westerland in 1855. Even then, quite a few bemoaned the advent of tourism.

Some islanders still harbour doubts. They'd rather have Sylt to themselves and deplore the high-rise building in Westerland, or the influx of tourists: nearly half a million day-trippers and overnight guests visit Germany's northernmost island every year and many old villas from the Wilhelminian era (the reign of Emperor William II, 1888–1918) were demolished to make way for apartment houses.

Guests that come to the island for some days or a couple of weeks have also doubled in number since 1980. But with its roughly 100 square kilometres of land, Sylt is the largest of Germany's North Sea islands, with room to spare and plenty of places off the beaten tourist track.

What makes Sylt so attractive?

One decisive factor is the landscape, with its mixture of sea, sand, lush meadows and village life – and the short distances between holiday bustle and splendid isolation on the long beaches. The sea is all around, and the sun rises and sets over splendid vistas of cloud and gleaming light, over stormy seas with crashing waves and over endless tranquillity. On cloudless days, the caressing warmth of the sun glitters on the masts of yachts rising from the quiet blue of the sea like the tall letters of an alphabet.

Many guests find themselves a quiet spot in one of the beach chairs, of which Sylt has an estimated 12,000. It's an ideal place to enjoy the sun whilst sheltering from the wind, alone or as a couple. Why not get on a bike and explore the island with the wind behind you or in your face (you can catch a bus back: in the tourist season, public transport dispenses with the need for cars). Surfers need to exert themselves a little more, leaping over the waves with paragliding sails.

A house on Sylt – a dream come true

Sylt has become increasingly popular as a holiday destination during the winter as well, especially around Christmas and

Above: A cottage thatched in Keitum. Centre: Winds and storms are constant companions on Sylt. Below: An attractive proposition. Spending money in Kampen. Right: The famous Red Cliffs near Kampen. Opposite page: Facing the mainland, part of the island near Munkmarsch.

the New Year, when long, quiet walks followed by mulled wine in the many inns and pubs are the order of the day. Some island-lovers have taken the extra step and fulfilled a life-long dream: a house on Sylt, preferably with a prettily thatched roof (at a price. For years now, thatching reeds have been imported from the Orient.)

Is Sylt an island for the rich? There are more than just a few holiday homes owned by the wealthy in Kampen and Keitum, but also in other island villages, where life is not quite so costly. People of vastly different backgrounds live here happily side-by-side – united by their love of the island.

The island came to public notice about 100 years ago, when artists began to visit during the summer. Painters such as Lovis Corinth and Heinrich Vogeler, writers including Gerhart Hauptmann und Thomas Mann, Stefan Zweig and Robert Musil, the 'rhyming seafarer' Joachim Ringelnatz and the redoubtable critic Alfred Kerr: they all made their way to the dunes and back to nature, relishing the chance to retreat from an urban working environment.

Peter Surhkamp wrote about Sylt: "It is never the same and yet unmistakably the same island. The way it presents itself always implies more than just its own natural self: there is always something else present. Those with memories of other, far-off places find traces here of an Homeric bay or a Scottish moor, a mountain valley or the Sahara, a 16th-century northern German village or – as somebody once claimed – even a Tibetan sky."

The fact that not much has changed may be attributed in large part to the dykes. Narrow as the island is – stretching from Hörnum in the south to List in the north – it's not always possible to

glimpse the sea and in certain spots it's quite feasible to look around and imagine a highland plateau, surrounded by mountain crests, even if the cliffs – such as the colourful Morsum Cliffs or the Red Cliffs near Wenningstedt and Kampen – are only 21 and 30 metres high respectively, the 55 metre-high Uwe Dune being the island's highest elevation. It was only in 1927 that the island was attached to the mainland by the Hindenburg Dam, as it is still known today, although the name now has a less of a positive ring. Since 1950s, car trains have rolled over the Hindenburg Dam on the Sylt Shuttle with ever-increasing ease. Just stick your credit card into the cash point, take your chip (valid for a return trip), wait a short while until the ramps are lowered, and drive onto the train. You can take everything you want with you in the car: fellow passengers, luggage, even bicycles, and drive off onto the island just 35 minutes later. For those in a hurry, there are flight connections.

There are lots of dreams tucked away in the suitcases crossing the water to Sylt every year: dreams that yearn to get away briefly from normal life, to be surrounded by the sea (even if it tends to be a little cool), by fresh air and wind, under the sun and the clouds. Most guests come from northern Germany, from North Rhine-Westphalia and Schleswig Holstein. Very few actually come from abroad. Returning to the mainland, you might remember what brought you in the first place: a specific kind of fascination with northern climes, far from southern seas, where you can cycle into the wind and delight in the clouds. Many visitors still dream this dream, but many others come in search of comfort and Sylt takes great care to provide it.

THE BEST PLACES TO EAT ON SYLT

It is one of the island's oldest hotels (founded in 1867) and since its extension in 2005 also one of the newest, with a splendid, clear view across the yacht harbour and the Wadden Sea: the ferrymaster's house in the former village of Munkmarsch, appointed with unassuming luxury. With one Michelin star and many other awards, it is also one of the best culinary addresses on Sylt, with a wonderful Victorian-style breakfast terrace!

Hotel and restaurant Fährhaus
Heefwai 1, 25980 Sylt-Ost/Munkmarsch
tel.: +49 (0)4651/93970, fax: 939710
www.faehrhaus-sylt.de

FOR MORE INFORMATION ON SYLT

Sylt Marketing GmbH
tel.: +49 (0)4651/82020, fax: 820222
websites: www.sylt.de, www.kampen.de, www.syltshuttle.de, www.flughafen.sylt.de

2 Eutin – Luxuriating in Lakes

Roses, poets and a castle

Nature parks are popular places with those who like to get away, at least now and then, from city life. Eutin, about half way between Lübeck and Kiel, was formerly home to a minor prince, one of many rulers of tiny fiefdoms that dominated maps of Germany. Nowadays, Eutin remains a medium-sized town, with a comparatively large market place. No high-rises, no parkways, but lots of roses – and it's never far to one of the three neighbouring lakes: the Grosser Eutiner See, whose waves lap up to the castle grounds, the Kleiner Eutiner See to the southwest and Kellersee to the north. All nestle in the green landscape, amid the woods and fields and the lakes of what is locally called Holstein Switzerland.

It was popular, during the early days of tourism, for the epithet "Switzerland" to be attached to local place names, in honour of any small elevations that might break the monotony of the surrounding lowlands – even if summits in the original Switzerland tended to be ten to twenty times as high. The landscape of Schleswig Holstein, washed gently by the surrounding sea, tends to be flat as a pancake – so the 168-metre high Bungsberg that rises from the gently rolling moraines left by retreating glaciers looks pretty impressive. These same glaciers also left behind the lakes. The flat landscape makes for pleasant hiking and cycling through the woods around Eutin. The two European long-distance hiking trails, the E1 and E6 that come from Schleswig and Denmark respectively, cross Holstein Switzerland in a south-easterly direction, as does the German holiday route from the Baltic Sea to the Alps. There is plenty to see in the vicinity: the Grosser Plöner See, beautiful old churches in Bosau and a late Gothic masterpiece, the carved altar of Bordesholm in the former Benedictine convent of Preetz on the Island of Bordesholm in Lake Eiderstedt – all evidence of local piety during the Middle Ages. There is a glassblowing workshop in Malente and a canoe rental for summer afternoons on the lakes. The sea is not far away either, in Sierksdorf, Scharbeutz and on the beach at Timmendorf.

Centre: rural idyll near Bosau. The local church has a valuable carved altar. Below: further east, on the edge of the Holstein Switzerland nature reserve, doors adorn cottages in Bockholt. Opposite, above: Grosser Plöner See – there are about 200 smaller lakes in the surrounding area. Opposite, right: Castle Eutin.

The imposing four-wing castle testifies to Eutin's historical importance. Its significance as a former fortified home to the bishops of Lübeck – from about 1270 onwards – is still evident. In fact, the whole building reflects local north German history: in the late 16th century, the Duke of Gottorf was elected Bishop of Lübeck. Renovations and a fire followed, before the dukes turned the castle and its park into a splendid 18th-century Baroque folly, complemented by English landscape gardens. Variously, the Dukes of Gottorf rose to become Kings of Sweden and Tsars of Russia. In 1773, the prince-bishops were given the title Duke of Oldenburg, later elevated to Grand Duke of Oldenburg. Full size portraits of these rulers look down upon castle visitors in felted slippers as they shuffle around the red, the blue, and the yellow salon, taking in the model ships, the silhouette portraits, and the tapestries.

For a long time, however, the now restored ceilings with their plaster mouldings sheltered bombed-out families from Hamburg, who were accommodated here for years after the war. Since 1992 the "Castle Eutin Foundation" has assumed responsibility for the freshly renovated building, offering a variety of interesting leisure opportunities that make the most of the castle and its gardens. Since 1951, Eutin has also held musical festivals celebrating the life and work of composer Carl Maria von Weber (whose birth house still stands in the Lübeckerstrasse 48). Friends of literature and antiquity remember Gottorf for employing Johann Heinrich Voss (1751–1826) as school headmaster in 1782, a posting that left the poet with plenty of time to translate the Odyssey and the Iliad. Voss stayed in Eutin for twenty years; his house is now a hotel. So it was through Eutin that Homer was introduced to Germany.

ON LAKE EUTIN

You will find the historic Voss house, with its restaurant "Da Vinci", its garden terrace and modern rooms, next to the castle and the castle grounds, almost directly on the shores of the Grosser Eutiner See.

Voss Haus Eutin
Vossplatz 6, 23701 Eutin
tel.: +49 (0)4521/40160, fax: 401620
www.vosshauseutin.de

FOR MORE INFORMATION ON EUTIN

Tourist-Info Eutin
tel.: +49 (0)4521/70970, fax 709720
website: www.eutin-tourismus.de

Centre: the steeper slopes of the Süllberg district are best negotiated via steps. Below: A view enjoyed by generations from the restaurant terrace atop the Süllberg. Opposite, above: Country villas and winding paths in Blankenese. Opposite, below: Upstream on the River Elbe, at the Teufelsbrück pier, with the Café Engel.

3 The Best of Hamburg

Blankenese and the Elbchaussee

There is something slightly reminiscent of the Mediterranean on the banks of the River Elbe in Blankenese – memories of Santorini or Taormina or other southern sites with steps and stairs. Where else in Germany is one forever tramping up or down? Blankenese, the old centre of this smart Hamburg suburb, nestles into the natural, semi-circular amphitheatre provided by the gently rising embankment. An astonishing number of houses – large and small – cluster on the slopes. In between: steps, more steps and yet more steps.

Building styles range from thatched cottage and half-timbered structures to villas from the Wilheminian era in whitewashed brick to steel and glass bungalows. But even the smallest of dwellings in this colourful conglomerate is framed by lovingly tended gardens. The flights of steps (each one of them unique) are made from natural stone and evoke the village life of bygone days.

Regardless of the style they chose, house owners all want one thing: a view onto the River Elbe upon which cogs and caravels, clippers and frigates once sailed upstream to Hamburg's harbour. Nowadays, the view is of container ships and tankers – but also of sailing boats and sometimes of cruise ships such as the "Queen Mary II". No wonder that seafarers choose, if they can, to retire here and observe the comings and goings on the river.

Blankenese used to be a fishing village. Local historians are full of tales from the time when the lands of Holstein and Lauenburg around Hamburg belonged to the Danish crown (until the German-Danish War of 1864) and Blankenese was home to the largest fishing fleet for miles around. In the 19th century, Blankenese-based shipping companies also ran a fleet of fast passage sailing boats that brought oranges from Mediterranean ports back to Hamburg before the onset of winter. In those days, however, Blankenese did not have its own harbour and in this respect at least, the sailing clubs on the riverbanks, with their strictly allocated moorings, are better off.

Splendid: Hanseatic greenery in the park

Obviously, such an exquisitely situated place has long since achieved a certain

KAPITAN NAZAREV
L 169

Above: Not far from the Elbchaussee: Jenisch House and Jenisch Park.
Centre: Snappily dressed ice-cream seller.
Below: From the River Elbe to Lake Alster, there is always something moving on Hamburg's waterways.
Opposite: Well-kept Blankenese, the houses of fishermen and sailors tucked away behind white fences.

cachet and it comes as no surprise to learn that Blankenese was an early beneficiary of technical advances, acquiring its own telephone system at the very outset of the Wilhelminian era in 1887, twenty years after its railway station. Further crucial dates include 1927, when Blankenese became part of Altona and 1937, when it was finally incorporated by the city of Hamburg.

Manor houses, mansions and villas began to spread themselves over the Süllberg, a small hill on the rim of Blankenese's "amphitheatre". At the same time, the first parks were laid out in the Oberland area of Blankenese, where they have remained to delight the eye ever since. The congestion of buildings on the slopes of the Elbe may feel a little close at times, but the lush greenery surrounding the mansions of Hanseatic traders more than compensates, with its generous vistas and splendid old trees.

Many old-established Blankanese families complain today about frequent subdivision and over-crowding on the formerly large plots of land. Nonetheless, many of the streets around Süllberg still evince the charms of gracious living and Blankenese remains Hamburg's most beautiful suburb. The Süllberg-summit, which lies 75 metres above the River Elbe, has recently received something of a facelift – at the expense of the cheerful hospitality that used to prevail. In 1837, a local innkeeper from Blankenese set up a refreshment kiosk here, expanding it shortly afterwards into an inn. The "silver terraces" quickly became popular with excursionists and partygoers of every kind. No visit to Blankenese was complete without a trip up the hill to enjoy the view across to the River Elbe. There is nothing stopping today's visitors from doing the same – except, perhaps, the price. The hotel straddling the hill today has risen to greater heights – of luxury, that is, and now includes a gourmet restaurant and a "private dining space", a ballroom and conference area. It's all a bit too much for many locals and shows scant regard for what the Baedeker guide describes as "over 150 years of painstaking attention to keeping the silver terraces in their original style."

All the more reason to appreciate formerly private parks that are now open to the general public, such as the Hirsch Park (Deer Park) with its magnificent showing of orchids, as well as Baurs Park and Gosslers Park. The area between Oberland and the River Elbe is still curtained with the woods that frame Blankenese, and it remains ideal for quiet rambles. Those familiar with the locality appreciate the Italianate settings of the "Roman Gardens" to the west of Waseberg, a little open-air theatre of lawns surrounded by hedges and, in summer, brightly coloured hollyhocks and gladioli.

Germany's richest road

Blankenese is part of greater Hamburg now and out-of-towners will find it hard to identify exactly where it starts – unless assisted by signposts or navigation systems. There is one exception, and one that all aficionados of the area are familiar with: the Elbchaussee, which leads directly from Blankenese to Altona. It was once called Germany's most

beautiful street, and one of those who coined the phrase was the poet Detlev von Liliencron. Cars were few during his lifetime. Today, vehicles stream up and down the five-kilometre avenue with almost the same persistence as the waters of the Elbe flowing below through the native sandy heaths. Understandably, the wealthy residents have let the hedges surrounding their properties grow higher and denser. Pedestrians and ramblers are best advised to take one of two specially landscaped trails: the Elbuferweg, down by the river, and the Elbhöhenweg, which runs through the hills slightly higher up. The view down over the river and into the marshlands beyond remains incomparable – albeit somewhat less so than in former years, before industrial plants in Finkenwerder (including those that produce the Airbus 380) supplanted the fruit trees.
The Jenisch Park in Klein Flottbek, situated on "Germany's richest road" is a monument to local philanthropy. Caspar Voght (1752–1839), one of Hamburg's foremost citizens, was a farmer and garden landscaper, much involved in reforming poorhouses. He chose a huge area near Klein Flottbek to create an exemplary agricultural estate based on English models. In 1928, with no heirs to succeed him, Voght sold the estate to the young banker and Hamburg City Senator Martin Johan Jenisch (1793–1857), who turned it into a true example of an English landscape garden. Since 1939, the park has been the property of the city of Hamburg; its neo-classical villa how houses a museum chronicling the affluent lifestyle and domestic culture of the people that built it. A second museum in the park was commissioned by the industrialist Hermann F. Reemtsma to be used for his extensive collection of work by the German sculptor Ernst Barlach, as well as for special exhibitions. More recently, the municipal environmental authority has worked to restore the park to its original appearance: the most beautiful part of Hamburg may soon be more beautiful still.

GROOMED BEAUTY

White Art Nouveau architecture, right on the promenade, an elegant if mature beauty about one hundred years old: these are the credentials of the Strandhotel Blankenese, with its 16 rooms and friendly hospitality. The beach is not suitable for swimming, but there is plenty of space on the narrow strip of gravel and greenery along the River Elbe for weddings and other champagne celebrations.
Strandhotel Blankenese
Strandweg 13, 22587 Hamburg
tel.: +49 (0)40/8662300, fax: 864936
www.strand-hotel.de

FOR MORE INFORMATION ON HAMBURG/BLANKENESE/ ELBCHAUSSEE

tourist information office in Hamburg's main station,
tel.: Hamburg-Hotline
+49 (0)40/30051300
Website: www.hamburg-tourismus.de

4 Hamburg's Latest Vision

Transition: from old warehouses to the new "HafenCity"

"Looking forward onto – not away from – the Elbe" is Hamburg's new motto. New plans envisage the extension of Hamburg's city centre to include the area down by the river where a new district is currently being developed: "HafenCity" (or port city), already fulsomely heralded as a "model for a 21st-century European city centre." It seems fair enough: no other maritime city in the area can boast such opulence. From the Inner Alster Lake, with its Venetian arcades opposite the Town Hall, to the Outer Alster Lake and its splendid villas; from the piers and the parks to the market places and the lakeside properties – the city centre is a well-tended paradise of prestigious living. Whatever is done is done in style.

Center: The warehouse district, seen here at Kehrwiederfleet. Below: Part of seafaring history, the shipping company Rickmer Rickmers. Opposite: Evenings at Brooktorkai can be solitary, but the HafenCity development aims to fill it – and the rest of the warehouse district – with new life.

Hamburg's port, with its adjacent industrial sites, is a highly potent economic motor, attracting hordes of tourists onto the cruise boats that tour the port area. But this is only part of the picture. The establishments that line the streets in the St. Pauli and Grosse Freiheit districts are less attractive – with a few notable exceptions situated on the Spielbudenplatz: pubs with their own specific musical traditions, or variety theatres and those devoted to local, folkloristic culture. And whatever happened to the former old town, with its network of narrow alleys that criss-crossed the district south of the Town Hall down to the harbour, around the churches of St. Catherine and St. Michaelis? Part of it fell prey to the urban renovation of the 1920s when it was torn down and replaced with modern developments. Most of these were themselves destroyed (with very few exceptions such as the Deichstrasse to the south of the Rödingsmarkt) during World War II.

The citizens of Hamburg decided to leave the ruins of St. Nicholas' Church standing – as a reminder of the atrocities of war. Prior to its destruction, it had been the third-highest church in Germany, after the Minster of Ulm and Cologne Cathedral. The severely bombed area around the church was put to new – and not exactly optimum use: in the absence of a definitive con-

Brooks-
Brücke
14

Above: Café at the InfoCenter in the Hafen City. Centre: freshly painted bridges. Below: Old warehouses. Opposite above: Freshly imported wares from the carpet weavers of the Orient. Opposite above right: A tea-taster, whose well-trained taste-buds are essential for Hamburg's tea-importers.

cept, it was cluttered with thousands of offices and carved up by multi-lane urban motorways. It was only in the 1990s that Hamburg's city government began implementing plans to beautify the city beyond the area immediately surrounding the Town Hall by gentrifying the district down by the port, and encouraging new developments in the port itself. It's easy enough to get there on foot and well worth the effort!

A world-class port in transition

Celebrating a port's birthday? Only in Hamburg where a festive procession of boats on May 7th marks the anniversary of Emperor Barbarossa's decision in 1189 to sign a letter of manumission exempting the lower Elbe from customs and excise tolls. Not all historians are convinced that the document is genuine but the port itself, which had only recently been founded, profited greatly from its existence, especially in the 19th and 20th centuries.

Some figures: the port currently occupies a total area of approximately 75 square kilometres, about ten percent of the overall acreage occupied by the Federal City State of Hamburg itself. Its most recent extension is the container port, for which the village of Altenwerder was fed to the bulldozers (despite protests by the inhabitants). Depending on the tides, the port can accommodate ships with a draught of up to 15 metres, directed into the channels by pilots and 12 radar stations on the lower Elbe. About 11,000 sea-going vessels from over 90 countries berth every year in Hamburg's port, one of the world's most important and efficient facilities in terms of rapid transition times (a 24-hour berth costs an average of EUR 15,000). The number of employees who work directly or indirectly for the port totals roughly 14,0000. Even still, large parts of the port are little more than industrial wastelands, with row upon row of disused warehouses and counting houses. Instead of tearing them down, Hamburg decided in 1991 to declare them protected monuments and halt their progressive dilapidation. Ever since, the picturesque neo-gothic structures, some of which can be up to eight floors high, form part of the harbour cruise itinerary.

Some of the warehouses have been transformed into niche museums: Spicy's Spice Museum opened its doors at the Sandtorkai, whilst a former carpet depot is home to the Museum for Afghan Art and Culture. The German Customs Museum at the Kornhausbrücke exhibits all manner of curious objects that were once considered taxable. The Miniature Wonderland occupies premises on Kehrwieder and boasts the world's largest digitally controlled model railway. The same house is home also to Hamburg's dungeon, where the city's history is told with special emphasis on the gruesome, such as the execution of the famous German pirate Klaus Störtebecker, the ravages of the plague, or the Great Fire of 1842. And last but not least, Dialogue in the Dark is a very special museum located on Wandrahm, where there is not much to see – but all the more to feel, smell and hear as visitors make their way through the dark with the help of visually impaired or completely blind guides.

Speicherstadt and HafenCity

The planners behind the "HafenCity" admit that it takes a bit of imagination to visualize the future port district: Following an interdisciplinary exchange of ideas and an international competition, the resulting master plan had to be sanctioned by the City Senate in the year 2000 before implementation could begin. "With amazement and delight we drove into the tumultuous chaos. [...] Here carpenters were at work; there some sailors were rowing boats and others were climbing up the masts [...] the muffled uproar of a thousand voices in hundreds of languages echoed around!" Thus did Joseph von Eichendorff describe his impressions of the port of Hamburg in 1805.
The new HafenCity district, which has been under construction since 2003, is made up of ten former city districts. It includes the area of the Grosser Grasbrook, the northern part of Grasbrook, a former island in the Elbe, and the Speicherstadt warehouse district on the former islands of Kehrwieder and Wandrahm. Separated by the Zollkanal, it borders on the inner city to the north, on the Elbe to the west and south, and on Rothenburgsort, separated by the Oberhafen, in the east. This district of Hamburg is completely enclosed by the river and canals and covers an area of some 2.2 km². It is planned that by 2025 the district will provide living accommodation for up to 12,000 people and workplaces for up to 50,000. The entire area along the waterfront as far as the Kehrwiederspitze, the former customs boundary of the Speicherstadt, has been completely re-planned. The Marco Polo and Magellan terraces curve gently round and down to the newly dug canal and its historic sailing boats. The outstanding attraction of HafenCity is Hamburg's new Elbphilharmonie, a concert hall built on top of Kaispeicher A, a gutted warehouse. The roof of Hamburg's new landmark is intended to represent a frozen wave.
Hamburgers hope that the new HafenCity district will fully reflect the city's traditionally cosmopolitan Hanseatic outlook and lifestyle. The Legislative Assembly governing this "green metropolis on the water" expects a better quality of life, and an increase in the city's international standing as an attractive investment proposition. It will take probably another decade. Time enough to take a look, now and then, at Europe's largest construction site.

HAMBURG'S MOST BEAUTIFUL STAIRWAY

Not far from the main station and – as the name Alsterblick suggests – with a view over the Outer Alster Lake and onto Harvestehude, this boutique hotel provides comfort and service in a one-hundred-year old building (recipient of the special award: Hamburg's Most Beautiful Stairway).

Hotel Alsterblick
Schwanenwik 30, 22087 Hamburg
tel.: +49 (0) 40/22948989, fax: 22948980
www.hotel-alsterblick.de

FOR MORE INFORMATION ON HAMBURG'S HAFENCITY

HafenCity InfoCenter
tel. +49 (0) 40/36901799, fax 36901816
Websites: www.hamburg-tourismus.de, www.HafenCity.info

Centre: A village shaped by artists and their work, exemplified here in a sculpture in the grounds of the Grosse Kunstschau gallery. Below: The House im Schluh, founded by Heinrich Vogeler's wife. Opposite: artists' wares for sale on local streets – from the earliest days of the colony to the present.

5 One Hundred Years on: the Worpswede Artists' Colony

Vogeler, Paula M. and Friends

To arrive is to feel at home, immediately. Because the streets and houses are flanked by high trees and surrounded by lots of garden greenery, because the village is vibrant but not loud. And a pleasant sense of anticipation hangs in the air: which paintings, which art works will we see? Some, perhaps, by the founders of the artists' colony themselves, or some by those who live and work in Worpswede today?

Let's start, then, with the house of one Heinrich Vogeler: Barkenhoff. Heinrich Vogeler, an artist from Bremen (1872–1942) came here in 1894, following the footsteps left a decade earlier by another artist, Fritz Mackensen. Vogeler shed the constraints of academic art in favour of the rough and ready landscape around a remote village in the Teufelsmoor (Devil's Swamp). The area was difficult to negotiate in those days, on sandy paths or in small barges. Vogeler bought himself a crumbling farm, and worked to turn it first into a dwelling and, over time, into an impressive artist's residence and family home with a terrace, a freestanding flight of steps, gardens and pavilion – a far cry from the original farmhouse.
Guests visiting Barkenhoff included the young and still-unknown poet Rainer Maria Rilke, whose short-lived marriage to the artist Clara Westhoff began here in Worpswede, and Paula Becker (1876–1907) from Dresden, who married the painter Otto Modersohn. Visitors to the newly and splendidly restored Barkenhoff can view a film biography of Vogeler. The artist's recently deceased son, Professor Jan Jürgen Vogeler, participated in its production, charting the rapid rise of the artists' colony following its founding in the year 1889. Only six years later, a joint exhibition in Munich's Glass Palace brought widespread recognition and new commissions.

Success, and the embrace of Communism

Vogeler was a multi-talented artist, painting landscapes and portraits that hover between Symbolism and Art Nouveau, as well as working as an architect

Reise Art

Above: No longer a place of dread: enticing waterways on the Teufelsmoor. Centre: Original country house. Below: Local meeting place: the Grosse Kunstschau gallery and gardens. Opposite below: a landscape of memorable natural charm.

and interior designer of furniture, porcelain, carpets and soon enough, and as one of the era's leading book artists, where his illustrations feature highly decorative arabesque whirls. After World War I, Vogeler felt called upon to devote himself more to social work. Having founded a commune in Barkenhoff, he later donated his home to the "Rote Hilfe" (Red Help Association), as a recreational home for children of the politically oppressed. He travelled to the newly founded Soviet Union, designed political posters and finally relocated completely to Moscow in 1931, taking his second wife with him. In 1941, he was evacuated to Kazakhstan, where he died in poverty. The exhibition of his work in House Barkenhoff shows the full range of his creativity, including the agitprop work of his Soviet years.

A simple imperative

Worpswede was home to other artists and some of their houses from the colony's early years are still standing. One such is the home of Paula Modersohn-Becker, the colony's most famous artist, who lived here with her husband in the small rooms of the Modersohn House on Hembergstrasse from 1897 until her early death after the birth of her daughter. In her portraits and still-life paintings, Modersohn-Becker sought to capture simplicity as a formal precept. An extract from her diary illustrates the intensity of her creative personality: "I feel so blessed. Is it not a gift, to be able to feel these splendours so deeply? … I wish to devote myself entirely to these feelings, in the hope that I may one day create something in which my soul resides … I say God, and I mean the spirit with which all nature is infused, and of which I, too, am a very small part." (24 January 1899)

An artists' colony: village and museum in one

Since 1994, the privately run "Modersohn-House Museum" owns and exhibits the Bernhard Kaufmann collection, which includes 15 paintings by Paula Modersohn-Becker. The paintings left by Otto Modersohn are not exhibited in Worpswede but in a half-timbered structure located in Fischerhude, about 15 kilometres to the south.
Visitors to Worpswede are likely to start their visit to the village at the former home of Vogeler's first wife Martha, who founded the "House in Schluh" in 1920. Since then, it has been run by her descendants, now in their fourth generation. Exhibits include works by Vogeler as well as temporary exhibitions. It is also possible to purchase handcrafted objects and take a room for a day or two.
No visit to Worpswede is complete without a look around the art gallery known as the "Grosse Kunstschau". Built by Bernhard Hoetger (1874–1949), the gallery is famous for its circular main hall. Hoetger is considered the father of expressive architecture, of which the Böttcherstrasse in Bremen has many fine examples, one of which is now home to the Paula-Modersohn-Becker House) Hoetger lived in Worpswede from 1919–33. His capriciously designed Café Worpswede, situated next to the Grosse Kunstschau is sometimes referred to by less tolerant locals as "Café Verrückt"

(Café Madness) – but this doesn't seem to bother Vogeler's sculpture of a Buddha entitled "Bonze des Humors" (Fat Cat Smiling), which sits between trees on the path leading to the Grosse Kunstschau, chuckling happily.
It would take days to go through all the art galleries and craft centres in Worpswede. Or to join one of the many painting, drawing, sculpture or pottery classes and explore one's own talents. The "Atelierhaus Worpswede e.V.", for example, provides stipends of three, six, nine or twelve-month residence courses to professional artists regardless or nationality or age. Then there are still the remains of the Teufelsmoor swamp to be discovered – now largely drained – where cotton grass and reeds ripple through the bog-birch forest. Boardwalks and cycle paths around Worpswede facilitate access to the swamp, either with or without professional guides. What about a trip up the little River Hamme under the red sail of a peat boat? The wooden benches take up to 16 people out on excursions between May and October.
Those with more time can invest a whole day, taking the "Moor Express", a heritage railway line first taken into service in 1909, to visit Stade on the River Elbe with its famous old town. Stade's Artists' House exhibits work from a number of European artists' colonies.
To relax: let's join Heinrich Vogeler again at Worpswede railway station, which he designed in the Art Nouveau style: the only one of Vogeler's stations on the Bremervörde-Osterholz line to have survived, later renovated and transformed into an atmospheric restaurant and inn. Musical publican Kai Holthoff keeps his guests entertained with live performances of music, from jazz to classical. Wallpaper and paint colours were selected on the basis of original plans from 1911. Vogeler's own etchings and part of the historic ticket office can still be seen.

EXPERIENCING ART NOUVEAU

Situated right next to Vogeler's Barkenhoff, a house named Buchenhof, in which the painter Hans am Ende (1864–1918) lived, is now a high-end bed and breakfast in which guests will find themselves surrounded by Art Nouveau antiques and original paintings. Situated on the edge of the forest with a private access road to the village centre and an in-house sauna and solarium.

Hotel Buchenhof
Ostendorfer Strasse 16, 27726 Worpswede
tel.: +49 (0)4792/93390, fax: 933929
www.hotel-buchenhof.de

FOR FURTHER INFORMATION ON WORPSWEDE

Tourist Information Worpswede
tel.: +49 (0)4792/935820, fax: 935823
websites: www.worpswede.de, www.barkenhoff-stiftung.de, www.kulturstiftung-ohz.de, www.artistsvillages.net

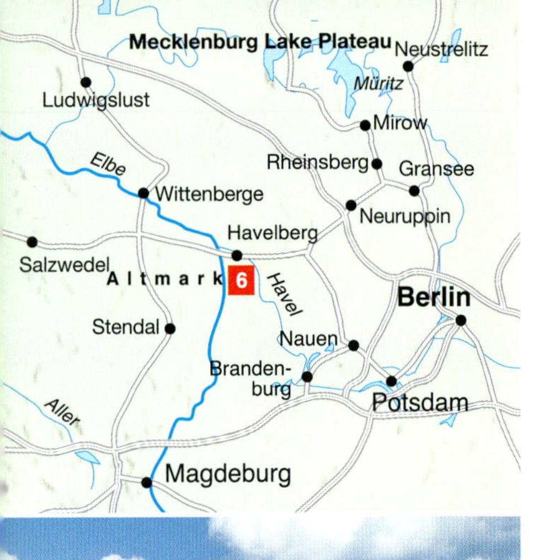

Centre: A landscape filled with tranquillity: Lake Arend to the northwest of Stendal. Below: Lots of room for pedestrians in Stendal's charmingly restored town centre. Opposite above: Away from the towns: fields and forests. Below: The former convent of Arendsee.

6 The Altmark Country around Havelberg, Stendal, Tangermünde

By the quiet waters of the River Elbe

Where a river is still a river, with oxbow lakes, with loops and meanders, where towns are small and their tallest building is still the church steeple – this is Altmark Country: an area to the north of the Brunswick-Magdeburg line, to the west of the River Havel, south of the River Elbe and east of Lower Saxony, this region forms part of Saxony-Anhalt and is known for its beautifully pristine landscape.

The local towns are small, none with a population of more than 50,000, as if following Otto von Bismarck's dictum that "large cities encourage revolution and should be razed from the face of the earth." Otto von Bismark, born in nearby Schönhausen, expressed this opinion in the Vereinigter Landtag (Regional Assembly) after the revolution of 1848, when he was still a lowly delegate, years before he rose to become Minister, Prime Minister and Chancellor. So instead of large cities, the region formerly contested by Germans and Slavs in many bloody battles now celebrates its natural beauty; Drömling Nature Park, home to otters and curlews: the Biosphere Reserve of the Elbe Meadows: the Colbitz Letzling Heath with its extensive network of footpaths: the European Bird Sanctuary on the River Milde: the area between the Rivers Elbe and Havel with its contrasting landscapes of low-lying reedy wetlands and gentle ridges formed by the Kammern Hills. Let's not forget the storks, which are everywhere in Altmark Country!

Havelberg: Hanseatic island town

And the towns: Havelberg, located partly on its own island in the River Havel. There is peace without, in the lands beyond the city, and within, in its Romanesque-Gothic cathedral, whose stepped gables, lofty nave and chiselled stone chancel belie its outer fortress-like structure. Havelberg first flourished as a medieval Bishopric and Member of the Hanseatic League but was still doing good business around 1900, when shipping on the River Havel experienced a peak and Havelberg had several shipyards and a port for steamboats travelling between Hamburg and Berlin. Once a year, Havelberg re-lives its glory days when over 250,000 visitors descend upon the town for the annual horse market.

Stendal – capital of the Altmark region – is also home to some superlative north German red brick Gothic. Visitors are welcomed by a moustachioed figure standing on the marketplace: Roland, a Frankish Knight, who rises here to a height of almost eight meters, Germany's third-highest version of the medieval hero who became a symbol of civic independence from the local nobility. This is a copy: the sandstone original was toppled by a storm in 1972, and given sanctuary in a museum. Everything else in Stendal is authentic, from the cobblestones and the colossal gates to the impressive oaks standing at the Tangermünder Gate.

Impressive façade

Tangermünde on the River Elbe, flowing northwards past the city, takes its name from the far smaller and practically unknown little river of Tanger. The town was once a fortress settlement, defending the Altmark region from the Slavs. Temporary residence of Emperor Charles IV, it was rebuilt after a devastating fire in 1617, and retains one of the best preserved half-timbered town centres in the area, watched over by the steeple of St. Stephen's Church and the red-brick keep on the banks of the River Elbe. The ornamental façade of the Town Hall is stunning, with delicately carved circular patterns. Down below the castle, built by Frederick I of Prussia around 1700, barges chug slowly up the quiet river. Further westwards, the verdant, lightly populated countryside stretches away to the Colbitz-Letzling Heath.

Cyclists can stretch their legs on the circular Altmark route, almost 500 kilometres long (the area has a total of 1,500 kilometres of cycle paths). Those who prefer water can rent rowing boats or canoes!

LIVING LIKE A KING

Hotel Schloss Schönfeld, situated to the west of Stendal, is a good regional base with its park, garden terrace and 14 comfortably appointed rooms, excellent cuisine and musical and literary soirees, as well as other events. Built in the late 19th century by the Rundstedt family, Schloss Schönfeld has been run as a hotel since 2001 by the brothers Ingo and Falk Bassenge.

Hotel Schloss Schönfeld
Schönfelder Strasse 1, 39599 Steinfeld
tel.: +49 (0)39324/98830, fax: 98831
www.hotel-schloss-schoenfeld.de

FOR MORE INFORMATION ON THE ALTMARK REGION AND STENDAL

Tourism Association of Altmark
tel.: +49 (0)39322/3460, fax: 43233
Tourist Information Havelberg
tel.: 039387/79091/19433, fax: 79092
Information Centre Stendal
tel.: +49 (0)3931/651190, fax: 651195
Websites: www.altmarktourismus.de, www.havelberg.de, www.stendal.

7 National Park in Western Pomerania's Bodden Landscape

Land and sea – a give and take

What is a Bodden? It's a saltwater marsh, a shallow bay in the Baltic Sea, separated from the open sea by peninsulas and islands. The processes of erosion or the accretion of soil can lead to changes, resulting either in the creation of new land or complete reclamation by the sea. The Bodden on the Baltic Sea are unique cold-water reservoirs, considered "essential to the gestation of marine life in the Baltic Sea" by conservationists.

Centre: lucky for the landscape of Darss that the much of the area around Zingst remained undeveloped – thanks to the nature reserve! Below: holidaymakers waiting for the obligatory boat trip. Opposite: Long beaches, white sand and walking trails through the high, grassy dunes – all especially beautiful in Ahrenshoop.

In their capacity as habitats in a constant state of flux, the Bodden are also invaluable refuges, stopovers for birds migrating north or south. The Western Pomeranian National Park once recorded up to 80,000 cranes during a migration season – a statistic unrivalled throughout Central Europe.

Founded in 1990, the Park covers an area of 805 square kilometres, from Cape Arkona on Rügen to the peninsula of Darss/Zingst, and up to Fischland and Ahrenshoop. But only about 15% of this area actually consists of islands or peninsulas. The rest is water or underwater biotopes in the Baltic Sea. About 50% of the land is forest; fields account for about 25% and the rest consists of beaches, dunes and reeds. Remember that settlements and surrounding areas, such as the popular towns of Prerow and Zingst and the villages on Hiddensee, are not part of National Park, which is like a huge nature reserve – accessible for visitors but not for investors looking to build hotels or inns. The Bodden landscape stretching from Hiddensee to Darss is divided into two protective zones: Zone I is largely exempt from commercial use, whilst the land in Zone II may be used "extensively for purposes of ecologically viable recreation and commerce."

A most charming island

"Hiddensee is a most charming island, quiet – so quiet. Let it not turn into some overrun spa!" wrote the poet Gerhart Hauptmann in 1899. The long, slender island – 16.5 kilometres in length and only between 125 and 3750 metres wide, lies in the sea to the west of Rügen; only its southernmost tip remains inaccessible to visitors, being

Above: Two rather squat lighthouses at Cap Arkona, on the northern tip of Rügen. Centre: Enough wind for colourful kites! Below: Prerow is quieter than Zingst – and is home to the museum of local natural history. Opposite: Bodden landscape near Zingst.

reserved entirely for birds. Gerhart Hauptmann can rest assured: one hundred years after noting his misgivings, the island itself remains largely as it was, without a promenade and large hotels. The number of summer visitors is impressive, though, totalling over 64,000 in August 2005. Those in search of the island's rough beauty amongst the broom and blackberry-covered hills to the north of Kloster, of solitary communion with the sea, the clouds and the special light should come during the off-season. The villages of Vitte, Kloster and Neuendorf attract most visitors: the village church in Kloster dates back to the 14th century and is the oldest building on the island. Towards the end of the 19th century, Hiddensee began attracting artists, scientists and writers such as Thomas Mann, who came with his wife, Katja, Albert Einstein and Sigmund Freud. Hauptmann himself visited the island 19 times. In 1930 he bought a house, "Haus Seedorn", now a museum. He is buried in the cemetery at Kloster.

Zingst and Prerow: cycling, rambling, swimming

Motor vehicles are forbidden on Hiddensee – except for the refuse removal. The Zingst/Darss area, on the other hand, site of countless holiday apartments and second homes in the villages of Zingst and Prerow, is easily accessible by car via the town of Barth. Thanks to a red-white turnpike barrier near Müggenburg, however, the entire eastern part of the peninsula, including mile upon mile of dunes, is reserved entirely for ramblers and cyclists. Forest paths are also off-limits to all "unlicensed use of motor vehicles". Ornithologists can indulge their interests in observation points and bird-hides, whilst swimmers delight in the fine, sandy beaches hemmed by a swathe of greenery. Cafés and cruise boats welcome less active visitors.

Prerow is quieter than Zingst, and the Darss forest much larger than that around Müggenburg. The dramatic geological events which gave rise to the Darss region are explained in Prerow's Darss-Museum – with special emphasis on the changing coastline: how soil depletion and accretion can be observed in the Darss area, how the northern tip of the peninsula has grown by 2.5 kilometres over the past 300 years. In the 15 years since its foundation, the National Park has devoted considerable resources to dismantling bunkers and other military sites left over on Hiddensee from World War II. Furthermore illegal holiday bungalows on Darss were torn down – along with an old factory, and Zingst was swept clear of munitions.

Ahrenshoop: artists' colony and holiday resort

Small is beautiful, says the local head of tourism – a popular sentiment in Ahrenshoop. He explains that it's better to grow slowly and sustainably, because it encourages care and respect when dealing with a geologically young environment. Visitors to Ahrenshoop come for pristine nature and a healthy climate – and the same goes for other towns in the narrow stretch of land known as Fischland.

Reed-thatched houses still prevail. The contrast between steep dunes and flat beaches, between the open sea and inland waters, the clouds in all colours of the rainbow and the bluest of oceans, the purple heathers and the grasses shimmering red in the evening sun, the splendid sunsets: all this creates a very special atmosphere on Fischland. Around the same time as one set of artists founded Worpswede, another group of painters discovered the charms of Fischland and set up their own Artists' Colony: The "Kunstkaten" (Art Hut) began its activities here in 1909 as "House for Local Arts and Handicrafts." It was the beginning of a long tradition, recently revived with a variety of galleries, exhibitions, concerts and readings, as well as a renowned annual art auction. Ahrenshoop is the epitome of prosperity without ever pandering to the latest trend or jeopardizing the homogeneous panorama with aggressively modern architecture. In addition to the Kunstkaten, new centres of artistic activity include a new auction house in Ahrenshoop and the "Strandhalle" (Beach House). The "Bunte Stube" (House of Many Colours) has sold and exhibited a variety of object including books and handicrafts since 1922, whilst the "LGM-Klanggalerie" (Sound Gallery), was built to emulate the shape of a human ear. Numerous private galleries supplement these more established institutions.

Cyclists, swimmers and ramblers can relax in the natural surroundings, including the native Ahrenshooper Holz, a kind of virgin deciduous mixed forest, about 450 years old, with giants ferns, thickly enmeshed blackberry brambles and holly, best treated with respect and encountered within the confines of a very brief foray.

NO STRESS PLEASE

A beautiful thatched house on the promenade with a view over the sea and the forest, a long stretch of beach just across the road: welcome to the Fischländer Hotel in Ahrenshoop, with a terrace, excellent cuisine and a wide selection of wines, a cocktail bar, many special getaway offers and one golden rule: stop the clocks and leave your stress behind.

Hotel Der Fischländer

Dorfstrasse 47e,
18347 Ostseebad Ahrenshoop,
tel.: +49 (0)38220/6950, fax: 69555
www.hotelderfischlaender.de

FOR MORE INFORMATION ON THE BODDEN LANDSCAPE OF UPPER POMERANIA

Nationalparksamt Vorpommersche Boddenlandschaft
tel.: +49 (0) 38234/5020, fax: 50224

Tourist Offices: Kurverwaltung Ostseebad Ahrenshoop
tel.: +49 (0)38220/66660, fax: 666629

Kur- und Tourismusbetrieb Ostseebad Prerow
tel.: +49 (0)38233/6100, fax: 61020

Kur- und Tourismus GmbH Zingst
tel.: +49 (0)38232/81580, fax: 81550

Websites: www.auf-nach-mv.de, www.bodden-nationalpark.de, www.nationalpark-vorpommersche-boddenlandschaft.de, www.ostseebad-ahrenshoop.de, www.ostseebad-prerow.de, www.zingst.de, www.kraniche.de

Centre: View of the painstakingly renovated old town. Below: The airy façade of the Town Hall on the Alter Markt, a masterpiece of brick architecture. Opposite: View over the old maritime city dominated by St. Nicholas' Church. Despite all the damage, there are still many gabled houses.

8 An Unexpected Beauty: Stralsund

Red-brick, blue seas, bridge to Rügen

In May 2003, the Lord Mayor of Stralsund accepted a document establishing the "historic old town districts of Stralsund and Wismar" as World Heritage Sites – one day after the President of the World Heritage Committee had presented the same document to the dignitaries of Wismar, where the situation following German re-unification had been just as catastrophic. Both cities had completed a long process of renovation and restoration – ably supported by the local populace, in particular, of Stralsund, where a citizens' committee was formed in 1991 with the declared intent to "Save the Old Town."

When 36 percent of a city's dwellings are completely uninhabitable and 43 percent are severely damaged, any city is likely to look ruined. By comparison, the remaining 21 percent (consisting of 17 percent lightly damaged and 4% well-preserved houses) tend to appear miniscule. These statistics, listed in the 1992 Annual Report of Stralsund's Urban Renewal Committee, summed up a situation caused by years of general neglect, lack of official support for house owners, lack of building materials as well as a preference for newer accommodation in prefabricated apartment blocks.

Today, Stralsund is one of eleven towns considered shining examples of urban renewal, the recipient of government and local state funding. Restoring the old town required huge efforts, without which World Heritage status might never have been granted.

Red and yellow brick façades line the streets of Stralsund, glowing in the sun (when it shines – which it does, according to statistics, more often than in Munich). The stepped gables are a typical feature, frequently subdivided into steep, ornamental arcaded apertures for windows. Some are crowned with small pointed caps, others flaunt Baroque curves. The last two of what were originally ten city gates – the Kniepertor in the north and the Kütertor in the west – remain as massive souvenirs from the Middle Ages. The Town Hall on the Alter Markt is an architectural landmark, with its late Gothic, pierced ornamental façade, flanked by two almost miniature historic gable houses and watched over by the mighty brick ashlars of

Preserving what was left, re-creating formerly vibrant districts down by the port Above and centre: View onto St. Nicholas' Church and the arcades on the marketplace. Below: The Maritime Museum will soon be supplemented by the "Ozeaneum". Opposite: Gables galore on the Alter Markt, with Gothic ogees and sensual Baroque curves.

The most important arguments in ravour of World Heritage status

The old towns of Stralsund and Wismar "represent an ideal version of Hanseatic League cities during its 14th-century heyday. Both towns have preserved their medieval layout ... and bear witness to the foundation of independent maritime trading centres based on the legal code known as "Lübisches Recht" (Law of Lübeck). The substance of the local buildings, and in particular, the six red-brick Gothic churches, attest to the political and economic significance, as well as the extraordinary prosperity enjoyed by both Hanseatic cities in the Middle Ages. In the 17th and 18th centuries, Stralsund and Wismar became important fortresses and administrative centres in the German regions under Swedish Governance and there remain many buildings from this era, testifying to their role."

St. Nicholas' Church which combine to create a truly unique setting of unexpected beauty.

Meeting place for the citizens: the Church of St. Nicholas

If architecture testifies to history then St. Nicholas' Church in Stralsund, the oldest parish church in the city, is a very special witness. Built around 1300 to emulate the Northern French Gothic cathedrals, it features the choir ambulatory typical of those churches. At that time, Stralsund was just beginning its rise to become one of the most important ports on the Baltic Sea, but was granted the special municipal self-government charter (Law of Lübeck) early on, in 1234. In the 14th century, at a time when the Hanseatic victory over Denmark was enshrined in the Peace of Stralsund, the city added a second tower to the cathedral, both topped by caps which were destroyed during a fire in 1662. The duress following the Thirty Years' War allowed for only one Baroque replacement. The unequal towers are now considered Stralsund's most prominent landmark.

St. Nicholas' Church was a place of worship, but also a place for the reception of foreign dignitaries, for council meetings and for the proclamation of new and important municipal laws. A devastating air raid in October 1944 laid waste to about one third of the old town, including forty old monuments. The damage inflicted on the church continues to occupy restorers. But it's been worth the wait: columns, walls and groin vaulting now dazzle visitors in their original, forceful colours complete with leafy ornamentation and blue and red painted bands. There are more recent touches too, such as the martyred figure of a corpse hanging, as if from a lamp post, on a modern crucifix.

Cobblestones and bird's eye perspective

Stralsund's old town welcomes pedestrians. Distances are short, and it's only a quick walk from town to port. Try viewing the city at different times of day and night, in summer, winter, or in snow (the local tourist office's wide selection of city walks includes a lamp-lit tour). Or why not take a scenic flight for a bird's eye perspective view of the city's almost triangular layout between surrounding stretches of water: the Strelasund to the north, separating the town from Rügen; the mainland lakes – the Knieperteich and the Frankenteich – dammed up in Middle Ages and accessible only via comparatively narrow bridges of land. It is still basically the same city structure as that laid down by settlers from the old imperial lands in the vicinity of a Slav trading post. Germany's latest and biggest feat of mechanical engineering is Stralsund's second bridge to Rügen – built to relieve the overburdened original. In the year of 2008 a major museum has been built in the port area: the "Ozeaneum", a new kind of maritime museum with gigantic tanks and interactive presentations.

During the GDR era, Stralsund and several neighbouring cities such as Rostock, Wismar and Wolgast, were highly productive shipbuilding centres (once occupying tenth place in Lloyd's Shipbuilding Register).

After the German reunification Stralsund's population sank by nearly one seventh (only 4,000 of an overall population of approximately 60,000 actually live in the old town). But for some years now, Mecklenburg-Western Pomerania has succeeded in establishing itself as a prime German tourist destination.

A VILLA IN THE PARK

Hotel An den Bleichen is an engaging bed and breakfast (restaurant in the house next door), surrounded by an extensive garden, not far from the old town in an elegant residential area close to the woods: 23 rooms, a generous breakfast buffet, a garden terrace, a sauna and a solarium; on-site parking.

Hotel An den Bleichen
An den Bleichen 45, 18435 Stralsund
tel.: +49 (0) 3831/390675, 392131, 392110, fax: 392153,
www.hotelandenbleichen.de

FURTHER INFORMATION ON STRALSUND

Tourism Centre
tel.: 03831/24690, fax: 246922
Websites: www.stralsundtourismus.de, www.stralsund.de

9 Müritz – and a National Park for Millions

The largest in the land of a thousand lakes

Extensive forests, shining lakes and first amongst these, Lake Müritz – the second largest lake in Germany after Lake Constance or, to be accurate, the German part of Lake Constance – surrounded by fields and meadows, villages and hamlets, copses, groves and majestic trees: welcome to the stunning natural landscape in the south of Mecklenburg-Western Pomerania as it was and now is again. Following decades of use as a military training ground by the Soviet Army, nature has proved that she can heal herself.

Centre: The little town of Waren on the northernmost shore of Lake Müritz is the largest settlement in the area and has several old churches and the Müritz Museum. Below: Sailing enthusiasts on Lake Müritz. Opposite: The beauty of the National Park forest.

Since 1990, a large part of the area has been part of the Müritz National Park. The lake itself is not part of the park: apart from a swathe of water 500 metres wide and heavily grown with reeds on the eastern shore of the lake. But there are plenty of other lakes in the park, the results of glacial snouts and melting waters from the last ice age, which filled depressions in the land: a typical topology found elsewhere in Germany but nowhere in such density as here, in an area comprising southern Mecklenburg and neighbouring Brandenburg from the Uckermark region to Ruppin Switzerland. Over one hundred lakes with an average surface area of more than one square hectare make water a principal attraction, popular with people – and with birds in general for nesting and also, in the case of ospreys, for hunting. 20 pairs of ospreys nest here, alongside about 14 pairs of white-tailed eagles. This splendid bird, known for a wing-span of 2.40 metres, builds aeries in mature pine trees able to support nests which can weigh up to 100 kilos. If you don't see an eagle, you'll almost certainly catch sight of a kingfisher with its impressive turquoise mantel over a rust-red gown. About sixty pairs of cranes come to the National Park to breed; the alder and birch fen woods, as well as damp areas in the process of silting up make for ideal breeding conditions providing tranquillity and protection from boars, foxes and humans. Nonetheless, cranes find their food in fields and meadows, and when they return, at the end of the day, to the breeding places in the National Park, their loud honking can be

Above: The small harbour of Rechlin, on the southern shores of Lake Müritz. Centre: endless vistas from the canoeist's perspective. Below: Sweetwater fishes from the lake! Opposite, above: Prettily restored: pedestrian zone in Waren.

heard for miles around, echoing through the evening skies.
There are three even larger nature reserves adjoining this one to the west, covering an area that reaches almost as far as Lake Schwerin and the Federal State Capital of Schwerin itself. To the east of the Müritz National Park, a fourth nature reserve covers the lakes around Feldberg, whilst another corner of the park also encompasses the area around Serrahn.

Discovering tomorrow's primeval forest

During the 19th century, the Grand Duke of Mecklenburg-Strelitz enclosed the large beech forest of Serrahn for use as hunting grounds, curtailing local lumbering. By 1952, when Serrahn forest was declared a nature conservation site, the woods had largely reverted to nature – a process now encouraged by the National Park administration. Humans are restricted to "watching and admiring" as the Grand Duke's former hunting grounds turn into tomorrow's jungle.

Visitors and their choices

Canoeists can choose between one of two water trails. One follows the upper courses of the River Havel from its source region near Kratzeburg through several lakes, ending in Great Lake Labus. The second trail begins on the eastern shore of Lake Müritz and follows a course through varied landscape via Lake Woterfitz southwards towards Lake Mirow. Some small sections are not navigable, but alternative means of boat transport enable easy transition at these points.

The National Park in Figures

How big is the Müritz National Park? Compared to the acreage of other German National Parks (excluding that of the Wadden Sea and the Bodden Landscape), this park is the largest in Germany. It's difficult to imagine an area the size of 43,810 football fields – or 322 square kilometres. Over two thirds of the park is forested, one eighth is water, just under one tenth consists of moor, only one twentieth of fields and meadows and a miniscule fiftieth is given over to farmland (about six square kilometres). Seen in the light of these statistics, the lake itself, with its 117 square kilometres, is not even that large.
More numbers? 54 species of mammal, 214 species of bird and 625 species of moth flourish in the Müritz National Park. And let's not forget the flora, with 133 species of moss and an impressive 593 different kinds of mushroom.

Boat (and bike) rentals are available at about ten different places. A bus service also covers the area, and there are bridle trails and paths accommodating horse-drawn carriages should the need arise. Setting out on foot is, of course, also an option. There are plenty of observation points and a nature-trail between Zinow and Serrahn, whilst dozens of themed tours are provided by the National Park Service. A very special

museum, the House of a Thousand Lakes dedicated to the lake and surrounding area, is located in the town of Waren on the northern shore, where a visitors' centre to be called the Müritzeum (Müritz Museum) concentrates specifically on Lake Müritz. Its extraordinary ark-like shape and wooden construction is worth its own visit. Recently, as many as 750,000 visitors have been registered each year. Young people in particular are encouraged to come to the park, with class outings and children's drawing competitions. There are also opportunities for student internships.

It's important to remember that this park, and many others, was enabled by the commitment and effort of environmentalists in the former GDR. The foundation of Müritz National Park – and that of 13 other protected areas – was officially promulgated on 12th September 1990 during the last session of the GDR Council of Ministers. The national park programme as a whole became part of the Unification Treaty. Its leading proponent in those days was Prof. Dr. Michael Succow, deputy Minister for the Environment in 1990, in the last GDR cabinet. Since 1992, he has held the post of Director of the Botanical Institute and Botantical Gardens of the University of Greifswald. In 1997, Michael Succow was awarded the "Alternative Nobel Prize" and used his prize money to found the "Michael-Succow-Foundation for the Protection of Nature".

HOSPITALITY À LA MECKLENBURG

It's hard to find more beautiful accommodation than that offered by the 17th-century Schlosshotel Gutshof Ludorf to the east of the little town of Röbel, with its extensive gardens and short walk down to the shores of Lake Müritz. The manor house itself has 23 rooms, the "Morizaner" Restaurant serves fresh local specialities, there is a garden terrace with beer garden – and also: sailing, canoeing, ornithological outings and house concerts.

Schlosshotel Gutshof Ludorf
17207 Ludorf/Müritz
tel.: +49 (0) 39931/8400, fax: 84620
www.gutshaus-ludorf.de

FOR MORE INFORMATION ON MÜRITZ NATIONAL PARK

Nationalparkamt Müritz
tel.: 039824/2520, fax: 25250
websites: www.nationalpark-mueritz.de, www.nationalpark-service.de, www.mecklenburgische-Seenplatte.de (re accommodation)

Centre: Rural delights around the castle of the Prussian Crown Prince.
Below: Small-town atmosphere still pervades most of Rheinsberg. Opposite: No Baroque folly, but substantial and beautifully situated directly on the shores of Lake Grienerick: Rheinsberg Castle as designed by future King Frederick II.

10 Rheinsberg, the Lake and the Castle

Where Frederick II spent his happiest days

The inhabitants of the little town to the north of Neuruppin in the Federal State of Brandenburg barely number 9,000 – yet the name is familiar. History buffs, and fans of Frederick II, know that he spent some years here, as Crown Prince, amongst friends, before shouldering the burdens of statehood as King of Prussia. Literature aficionados may know the little "Rheinsberg: A Picture Book for Lovers". Written by Kurt Tucholsky and published in 1912, it marked the beginning of his literary career. Difficult to believe that such a coolly defiant and unapologetically erotic tale could have been written during the prudish Wilhelminian era. It's a shame that having tried without success to sell the book, Tucholsky was forced to accept a miserable 125 Reichsmark from publisher Axel Juncker and was unable to profit from the its unexpected success.

Different as they were, these two men had one thing in common. Both the young Frederick, future King of the Prussians who spent four years in Rheinsberg, and Kurt Tucholsky, who came here by rail from Berlin as a 21-year-old law student on a weekend jaunt with his girlfriend Else Weil, experienced the castle, the lake and the park as a place of recreation and rest. The local landscape is beautiful enough in its own right, but visitors to Rheinsberg come in the expectation of something really special. They are seldom disappointed. The sun shines as the pleasure boats chug across the lake, visitors to the castle gardens seek the cool of shady corners, and diners on a restaurant terraces indulge in a glass of wine to round things off. What more could one ask?

The crown prince, the castle and the king

One important advantage enjoyed by Rheinsberg Castle is its lakeside location

Summer days around Rheinsberg Castle. Above: Plenty of space to sit and chat under majestic ionic capitals. Centre: Cyclists take a break on the lake shore. Below: Reaching for water at the pump.

on the site of a former 16th-century moat-castle. The famous German author Theodor Fontane describes it concisely in his travel writings: "The castle was originally a Gothic structure with a tower and a pitched roof. It was only in the early years of the last (18th) century that a new castle in the French style replaced the older Gothic building. Thirty years later, the architect Knobelsdorff oversaw the completion of this new castle, creating the ensemble that we see today, consisting of a main central section and two wings connected by a colonnade facing onto the lake." (Rambles through the Brandenburg March, vol. 1, 1862)

The architect Georg Wenzeslaus von Knobelsdorff (1699–1753) was a friend of Frederick, but his participation in restructuring the castle was anything by self-evident. The crown prince and his father, the King of Prussia, were deeply estranged. In fact, Frederick once attempted to flee his father's reach of power in an abortive episode also involving his best friend Katte. Both he and Katte were arrested, and Katte was subsequently executed in front of Frederick's very eyes. Frederick himself was beaten until he bled by his father and also threatened with death, but his sentence was commuted to imprisonment in the fortress of Küstrin. It was only once he had agreed to submit unconditionally to his father's will, swearing upon oath to obey his orders to the letter, that he was allowed to leave prison. And it was only once he agreed, very much against his own inclination, to marry a princess from the House of Brunswick and had served as an officer in the garrison at Ruppin, that a superficial reconciliation was effected. King Frederick William I gifted Castle Rheinsberg to his son, but instead of employing Frederick's architect of choice, the king initially awarded the commission to the master builder Johann Georg Kemmeter.

Frederick reacted diplomatically by sending his friend Knobelsdorff to Italy to study Palladio's villas before appointing him as the principle architect of Castle Rheinsberg in 1734 – this time, with the agreement of his father. Knobelsdorff's great architectural coup was the lakeside addition of a double row of ionic columns, forming a colonnade that efficiently connected the tower library with the hall of mirrors, also used as a concert hall.

Knobelsdorff's years in Rheinsberg sowed the seeds for his later successes. When Frederick came to power, Knobelsdorff was promoted to the rank of Superintendant in charge of Palaces and Gardens. He built the new wing on Charlottenburg Palace in Berlin, the Opera House on Berlin's Unter den Linden, the Palace of Sanssouci in Potsdam and much more, before dying, relatively young, at the age of 54.

"Serious matters have priority..."

From 1736 onwards until the death of Frederick William I, Crown Prince Frederick lived mainly in Rheinsberg, where he may have occasionally have been disturbed by construction work – but not by his wife, Elisabeth Christine, who lived in her own apartments separate from those of her husband. The time they spent in Rheinsberg was actually

the only time they lived under one roof. They had no children and when Frederick became king, he sent his wife off to live by herself.
Frederick devoted himself to music, literature and state philosophy. The Prussian court painter Antoine Pesne from Paris (1683–1757), a master of the gallant portrait and gracious dancing scenes, was given the task of decorating the modernized castle. The most famous of his achievements in Rheinsberg was the ceiling fresco for the Concert Hall, completed in 1739. Based on a story related by Ovid, the fresco shows the rising sun, whose rays dispel the darkness. Many visitors, as Fontane noted, preferred their own interpretation: "Young Prince Luminous ousts King Grumpy." The Young Prince Luminous was well aware of the challenges awaiting him and made full use of every hour spent in Rheinsberg: "We have divided our occupations into two categories; firstly, the useful and secondly, the pleasant. I count the study of philosophy, history and languages as useful. The pleasant pursuits are music, comedy and drama, which we ourselves act ... Nonetheless, the useful occupations have priority, and I dare say that we take only limited recourse to the pleasant ones."
Whilst in Rheinsberg, Frederick wrote the "Anti-Machiavelli Manifesto" declaring his support of enlightened absolutism, viewing himself "the foremost servant of the state." He began to correspond with the French philosopher Voltaire. Inviting Voltaire to Berlin was one of the first things he did as King. Most of the rooms have been restored to their original splendour, complete with mouldings, ovens and golden cherubs. The historic gardens are also once again resplendent with a grotto and an obelisk, marble statues and an orangery with pavilion. Kurt Tucholsky, the master of biting satire, the pacifist and social critic, also have his own museum and memorial in the grounds.

FOR MORE INFORMATION ON RHEINSBERG

Verkehrsverein Rheinsberger
Seenkette e.V.
tel.: +49 (0)33931/2059, fax: 34704
websites: www.ruppin.de/Rheinsberg

Centre: Water games in Sanssouci Park. Below: Lightly clad, roguish Rococo sculptures on the garden façade. Opposite: The New Palace and the Chinese Tea House in Sanssouci Park. Below: Idyll on Peacock Island, an antique-style temple in the middle of Brandenburg.

11 Castles on the River Havel: from Berlin to Potsdam

Prussian arcadia

It's just a small river, but there are beautiful buildings on its banks. Geographically speaking, the first castle is just a ruin now, situated on the Pfaueninsel (Peacock Island). Politically speaking, the island still forms part of Berlin. From a cultural point of view, it forms part of the Prussian arcadia that grew up around the formally insignificant little town of Potsdam.

The Great Elector of Brandenburg set the course in 1660, when he chose Potsdam as a second residence after Berlin. Surrounded by water and woods, the location was ideal for hunting and close to Berlin: features which today's commuters between Potsdam and the capital still appreciate. Johann Moritz von Nassau-Siegen, the Great Elector's Proconsul in the Rhenish provinces, pointed out Potsdam's advantages in a letter written to his master in 1664: the island, he wrote, meaning Potsdam, "will doubtless become a paradise". The ruling Hohenzollern dynasty spent the next 250 years or so trying to fulfil this prophecy – right up to November 1918, when Emperor William II abdicated and went into exile in the Netherlands.
The Hohenzollern participated actively in nearly all the construction and landscaping work carried out in the area and much of it feels intimately familiar. Their interest was not limited to castles and palaces but included buildings such as the log cabin Nikolskoe, which lies on the road leading down to the Pfaueninsel ferry landing. When King Frederick William III (1770–1840) met with his daughter Charlotte and her husband, Tsar Nicholas I, in a Russian log cabin outside St. Petersburg, he enjoyed himself so much that he had a copy of it built to surprise the couple when they visited Berlin in 1819. The colourfully ornamented cabin remains a favourite destination with day-trippers from Berlin, – although significantly reconstructed after a fire in 1984. Two famous German architects, August Stüler und Albert Dietrich Schadow, designed the neighbouring Church of St. Peter and Paul, complete with onion domes and Romanesque arches (1834–37).
The enchanting castle and grounds on Pfaueninsel (Peacock Island) were not strictly a family affair. For a long time, the island was simply named Kanin-

Above: To the west of Potsdam, green farmlands on Lake Zern.
Centre: Exotic and costly: the Chinese Tea House in Sanssouci Park.
Below: Detail, garden pavilion.
Opposite: "Sans Souci", free of care is how Frederick II wished to live in his palace, but one war after the next soon put an end to the idyll.

chenwerder for the rabbits bred there in accordance with the Great Elector's wishes. There followed a period of residence by the alchemist and glassmaker Johann Kunckel. Frederick William II (1744–1797), the nephew of Frederick the Great, first used the island to hunt and then transformed it into a love nest for his life-long mistress and confidante, the perspicacious Wilhelmine Encke, later Baroness Lichtenau. His assistant in this enterprise was the famous garden architect Peter Joseph Lenné. Together they created an exotic park, home to the eponymous peacocks. The island castle was constructed in the romantic ruin look, with a cast iron bridge between the towers.
King Frederick William II died relatively young, aged 53. His son, Frederick William III was a serious-minded young man, known for his conservative taste and diligence. When it came to dealing with his father's mistress, Baroness Lichtenau, he displayed less estimable qualities, ordering her imprisonment without proof of wrongdoing and her complete dispossession. Lack of finances restrained castle building during this era, but the king and his wife, Queen Louise, spent happy hours on the Pfaueninsel.

The royal progeny and their castles

Yet Frederick William III left some traces in Prussia's arcadia after all – through his children: Crown Prince Frederick William (1795–1861), later King Frederick William IV, was given land in the park around Sanssouci Palace, where he built himself the classically inspired Charlottenhof Palace and Roman Baths. Second-born William (1797–1888), who reluctantly allowed himself to be crowned German Emperor in Versailles aged 74, received the Babelsberg grounds, opposite the Glienicke Hunting Lodge. Babelsberg was an extensive landscape park, designed by two of Germany's most influential garden architects: initially by Lenné, and subsequently by Prince Pückler-Muskau. In 1833, construction of a new castle began, based on preferences expressed by William's wife Augusta and the plans of the era's greatest German architect, Friedrich Schinkel. The design called for a castle in the English neo-Gothic style with a view over Lake Tiefen, Lake Glienicke and Glienicke Bridge (which became famous during the Cold War, when spies and prisoners were exchanged between East and West).
The third-born son Carl (1801–1881) was also given land by his father: the manor and surrounding grounds to the east of Glienicke Bridge, formerly the property of the Chancellor, Prince Hardenberg. Again, it was the tireless Schinkel who planned the transformation from manor house to summer palace. Carl and his wife, Marie von Sachsen-Weimar, were delighted with Klein (Small) Glienicke: a neo-classical gem surrounded by gardens designed by Lenné. These same gardens are now a public park. Whether you come on foot or drive by on the Königsstrasse heading for Glienicke Bridge and Potsdam, there is still plenty to admire, not least the golden griffins and lions that remain as evidence of past glories.
There was space enough for all these palaces and castles in the verdant mead-

ows by the area's many rivers and lakes. Each had its own landing and the various princely courts regularly spent days down by the water, admiring the view onto bays and coves and idyllic islands. Small wonder that courtiers and men of wealth and influence bought the adjacent plots, settling as close as they could to the ruling family. Elegant residential areas developed on the banks of Potsdam Island.

The whole area bears witness to the harmony that can be achieved between land and water, between extensive parks and exceptional architecture – and nowhere is it more evident that on and around Heiligensee, an area between the affluent Potsdam suburbs known as Nauener Vorstadt and Berliner Vorstadt. Frederick the Great died childless, and was succeeded by his nephew, Frederick William II, who had the Neuer Garten (New Garden) bordering on Lake Heiliger designed along the lines of Wörlitz Park (see page 74). The jewel in the crown of these grounds was to be the Marble Palace, but funds ran out and the architect was forced to dismantle the marble colonnades in nearby Sanssouci Park and re-cycle them for the new Marble Palace. The last of the palaces was built between 1913–17 in the area to the north of the New Garden for William, son of the last German emperor, and his wife, Cecilie von Mecklenburg-Schwerin. Built in the English Tudor style, it is more of a manor than a palace. Today, it is a hotel. Visitors to the palace can still see the conference room in which Truman, Stalin and Churchill (later Attlee) negotiated the Potsdam Agreement in the summer of 1945.

Frederick II chose the area of Potsdam as a refuge from state affairs, and Sanssouci Palace, built in 1745 by Knobelsdorff, has all the hallmarks of a retreat, with its park, its vineyard terraces and the small buildings dotted around the grounds. Sanssouci remains the most personal of all the palaces in Berlin and Potsdam to have acquired World Heritage Site status, a unique and charming monument to Frederick's personal predilection for Rococo, although it is not situated on the river but on a local canal. It was shortly after German re-unification that the palaces (including the Pfaueninsel and Glienicke Palace) were declared World Heritage Sites.

WHERE GUESTS ARE TREATED LIKE KINGS

The old-established Hotel Am Jägertor with its classical atmosphere is conveniently situated close to Potsdam's centre and makes a point of treating its guests like kings. Good cuisine. The in-house garage helps avoid parking problems and the hotel offers a multitude of special arrangements. Member of the Travel Charme Hotels.

Hotel Am Jägertor
Hegelallee 11, 24467 Potsdam
tel.: +49 (0)331/2011100, fax: 2011333
www.tc-hotels.de

FOR MORE INFORMATION ON POTSDAM

Potsdam-Information
tel.:+49 (0)331/21100, fax: 0331/23012
Websites: www.potsdam.de,
www.berlin.de/tourismus/sehenswuerdigkeiten, www.schiffahrt-in-potsdam.de

Centre: view eastwards from the Reichstag cupola, with television tower on Alexanderplatz. Below and opposite, above: up the spiral walkway to the uppermost platform, a magnet for thousands of visitors every day.
Opposite below: Office of the Federal President and the Congress Hall, known today as the "House of World Cultures."

12 Central Berlin: The Tiergarten Park and Reichstag Cupola

Green forecourt and transparent skies

Berlin's Tiergarten Park is more than just a green lung in the middle of a metropolis: it is both geographically and historically central, reflecting directly on events of the past 100 years. Four years after the end of World War II, after the blockade and the airlift, the grounds were ruined: bombarded, dug up and deforested. Forty years later, a new landscape park had been created, based on the original plans of the garden architect Lenné, and it's almost as if the clock had been turned back to the times of Emperor William: over one million trees and shrubs were planted, old statues returned to commemorate Frederick William II and the enchanting Queen Louise, the celebrated German writers Goethe und Lessing, or political and military leaders such as Bismarck and Moltke.

And today? Now that the Tiergarten no longer sits in the shadow of the Berlin Wall on the outer fringes of West Berlin but in the middle of a newly revived government district, it forms a leafy passageway from central Berlin and its sites – the Museum Island, the parliamentary headquarters in the Reichstag, and the Brandenburg Gate plus the magnificent old boulevard Unter den Linden – to the districts in western Berlin. 25 kilometres of footpaths welcome strollers to the peace and quiet of a spacious park, for exercise, meditation, rowing on the Neuer See, a coffee or a beer on its shores. 400 years ago, these were the hunting grounds of the local ruler. As a 19th-century park, it was opened to the newly developed class of citizens who enjoyed strolling through trees and over grassy meadows, lingering on bridges and on lakeside benches. Situated in the centre of Germany's roaring capital, today's Tiergarten is more than just an oasis. Just ten minutes from the Reichstag, seat of the German parliament, the Congress Centre (built 1957–58) is home to the "House of World Cultures" which, as the name suggests, stages a

Berlin. Das Mexiko-Fest

Above: symbol of a divided city, the sculpture entitled "Berlin" on Tauentzien Street, the work of Matschinsky-Denninghoff. Centre: Still waters in the Tiergarten. Below: Potsdamer Platz. Opposite: A costly renovation restored the Brandenburg Gate too its former glory. Opposite right: The Siegessäule, inaugurated in 1873.

wide range of events. And not much further on, cocooned in the depths of its own garden, the newly renovated neo-classical Bellevue Palace is the residence of the Federal German President. The Strasse des 17. Juni is a continuation of Unter den Linden, which intersects with major north-south axes at a point known as Der Große Stern (large star) at whose centre a winged statue stands triumphantly atop a column. This is what Berliners refer to irreverently as "Golden Else", a figure from a famous German fairy story. The 285 steps to the look-out platform afford a stupendous view, out over the Tiergarten and the neighbouring Culture Forum, and further still, over embassies and villas right up to Berlin's famous zoo, formerly part of the Tiergarten. Looking eastwards, observers will note the massive Soviet memorial, erected in 1945 with materials taken from Hitler's Imperial Chancery and behind it, the familiar forms of the Brandenburg Gate and the Reichstag building.

The cupola: Norman Foster's compromise

The seat of the German parliament, the Bundestag, has retained the name it bore when it was built according to the plans of Paul Wallot in the late 19th century. Its walls have witnessed great changes, from the pompous confidence prior to World War I, to the brief flowering of democracy after the war (on November 9th 1918, Philipp Scheidemann proclaimed the foundation of a "German Republic" from a window in the building's western façade), and on, unhappily, to the abuse and downfall of democracy when the building was torched in February 1933 and used as a pretext by Hitler for persecuting his political foes. At the end of World War II, the irrevocable conquest of Berlin was signalled by Soviet troops storming the Reichstag: the rhetoric of their victory is still there today in the graffiti left on the walls. For years, the building was left as a topless ruin: the steel framework of the original cupola had been detonated before undergoing some superficial restoration in the 1960s. But it was only restored to its full function as home to the German parliament after re-unification.

British architect Sir Norman Foster won an international contest to restore and partially redesign the Reichstag – a fitting choice in view of the building's history. After some initial differences, Foster fell in with the wishes of his clients – the German Parliament's Council of Elders – and many other leading German personalities and drew up plans for a new cupola. His vision epitomized the concept of transparent democracy: a glass cupola symbolizing a forum in which a sovereign people mingles with its parliamentary representatives. Right from the start, the architectural crystal was considered a huge success. Berliners and out-of-towners alike came and continue to come in their thousands, streaming up the spiral walkway to the cupola's top platform where Berlin is spread out all around in a spectacular 360-degree panorama view: the river, the television tower, Unter den Linden and Berlin's main cathedral, the Tiergarten and the new skyscrapers on Potsdamer Platz, the elegant residential district of Charlotten-

burg and the old radio tower beyond. On clear days, the view extends far out into the surrounding countryside.
The cupola also has a restaurant with limited seating, and on sunny days, al fresco dining is possible – albeit in a stiff breeze.

"You can't take it apart"

Foster designed the cupola to include an inverted cone in the middle, on which 360 inclined mirrors reflect light into the building's interior. Visitors walking up and down the cupola walkways can observe themselves as refractions – an interesting perspective that many linger over. The cone's lower point actually intrudes into the parliamentary plenary hall, like a large spindle. It houses the ecologically efficient ventilation and heating systems: ventilation takes place through the cupola, the building is heated with biological fuels. A heat accumulator at a depth of 300 metres gathers energy produced by solar panels. Asked about his concept, Norman Foster once said: "… You can't remove any one part of it without irreparably damaging the philosophy behind it. If visitors were not permitted access, the building would not feel like a public space, a social forum. If we hadn't used glass, and allowed daylight into the building, our energy concept would have proved unrealistic: we need the sun for our heating system. If hot air were not allowed to escape from the cupola, it would soon get very warm. Everything is connected. The Reichstag is like a person. It has a heart, good sense and a body: every bit is co-dependent on the others."
Many visitors to the building remain unaware of these interdependencies. They are happy to walk up into the sky that surrounds Reichstag, 460 metres up and down: one of Germany's most beautiful footpaths.

ELEGANT AND IMAGINATIVE DESIGN

Visitors who don't mind spending a little more on their visit to the capital will feel right at home in the Brandenburger Hof hotel: an old town house, not far from the zoo and the upmarket stores on Kurfürstendamm.

Hotel Brandenburger Hof
Eislebener Strasse 14, 10789 Berlin
tel.: +49 (0)30/214050, fax: 21405100
www.brandenburger-hof.com
Member of the Small Luxury Hotels Group

FOR MORE INFORMATION ON BERLIN

Tourist Info Centre
Brandenburg Gate/side wing
Websites:
www.berlin.de/tourismus/sehenswuerdigkeiten, www.berlin-tourist-information.de, www.bundestag.de

Fine sands for bathers and sun-worshippers: Spiekeroog has plenty to offer – from dunes to conifers. Where else might one find a museum dedicated to shells?

13 Spiekeroog

One of seven sandy beauties

The sea and the wind joined forces to create the "Seven East Frisian Sisters": a group of sandy islands forested with pines, one of which is "Spiekeroog". The seven sisters are located in the Wattenmeer National Park where they enjoy nature reserve status. Further characteristics include the typical Frisian villages, which stand out amongst more recent constructions, and the much-vaunted high-quality sand. Casinos and congress centres are not needed here. Instead, the great outdoors beckons, with beach life, sailing and surfing, riding and cycling. Horses still pull the old traditional trams, "the very first German horse-drawn tram" over narrow tracks. The car-free island measures 17 square kilometres and is just one hour's ferry-ride away from the harbour of Neuharlingersiel. Perfect for those in search of peace and quiet, and maybe gentle recreation like readings, discussion evenings. Spiekeroog has a lot to offer.

HOTEL RECOMMENDATION: Hotel zur Linde, Norderloog 5, 26474 Spiekeroog, tel.: +49 (0)4976/91940, fax: 919430, www.linde-spiekeroog.de

14 Königslutter and the Elm Region

Deciduous forest and Lombard architecture

Before re-unification, cars waiting to cross the inner-German border at Marienborn could at least enjoy the view over beech forests and the scent of sweet woodruff-part of the Elm-Lappwald nature reserve. The reserve also covers the Rieseberg Moor with rare orchids and extends southwards as far as Schöppenstedt, and also comprises Helmstedt, the Tetzel Stone (where a knight is purported to have robbed a seller of indulgences) and Königslutter. Emperor Lothar commissioned the Romanesque collegiate church, in which he was buried in 1137. The church was built by Lombard stonemasons and features the characteristic three-nave construction with elaborately ornamented columns, a lion portal and hunting frieze around the apse. The alleys around the church complement the medieval atmosphere.

HOTEL RECOMMENDATION: Comfort garuanteed in the Avalon Hotelpark Königshof. Braunschweiger Str. 21a, 38154 Königslutter am Elm, tel.: +49 (0) 5353/5030, fax: 503244, www.hotelpark-koenigshof.de

15 On Tree-lined Roads

Under a green and golden canopy

Germany's Alleenstrasse is a succession of tree-lined country roads, stretching Rügen in the north on to the Hanseatic town of Stralsund, the Mecklenburg Lake Plateau, and the towns of Eisenach, Fulda, Torgau, Meissen, Halberstadt and Goslar with tributary roads branching off into regions as far south as Lake Constance. Its aim, however, is not to merely to connect but to invite travellers to look and enjoy, whether travelling by car, by bike or on foot. Tree-lined country roads are much more common in the north and east of Germany than in the west and the south, where much replanting work is currently under way after years of cutting back trees to make space for the wider roads needed for Germany's economic miracle. The Deutsche Alleenstraße e.V. is actually a registered society dedicated to restoring tree-lined country roads to their original beauty, bringing them to public attention and conserving them as part of Germany's national heritage. Travellers use the roads to explore Germany region by region. The society's has guide accommodation tips and maps.

Travelling by car down Germany's tree-lined roads takes longer – and so it should. Take time to enjoy the shade.

16 Jasmund National Park

The lure of the Königsstuhl

The German Romantic painter Caspar David Friedrich, a master of atmospheric landscapes, executed the ultimate Rügen painting: the world-famous "Chalk Cliffs on Rügen". Nearly 200 years have passed and time and erosion have effected changes the strange chalky outcrops rising from the sea. Nobody knows exactly which cliffs Friedrich painted: those at Wissow, at the Viktoria Viewing Point or maybe in Klein-Stubbenkammer. The Baltic Sea is wearing down the island's coastline; rocks and trees sometimes tumble into the ocean. The region has been a nature conservation area since 1920, and in 1990 it was integrated into the 30 square kilometres that form the Jasmund National Park so that the scene painted by Friedrich is protected from industrial use at least. Millions wish to see the chalk cliffs with their own eyes: the viewing platform at the Königsstuhl registers 500,000 visitors a year.

HOTEL RECOMMENDATION: Parkhotel Sassnitz, Hauptstrasse 36, 18546 Sassnitz, tel.: +49 (0) 38392/6950, fax: 695199, E-Mail ParkhotelSassnitz@t-online.de

The chalk cliffs alone make a trip to Rügen worthwhile.

Countless castles, charming villages with half timbered houses, and innumerable parks nestle in the picturesque river valleys and dense forests of the regions known as the central German uplands. Right: location is everything – the Concordia Water Palace in Bamberg.

Germany's Centre

17 Münster and the Münsterland

Moated castles and other wondrous things

There are plenty of places in Germany where history comes alive in architecture, such as the Brandenburg Gate and the Reichstag in Berlin. Another is the Wartburg fortress where Martin Luther sought refuge from enemies, using his time there to translate the New Testament into German. Münster has two, maybe three such locations: places where history turned and new developments began.

Centre: home of the Droste-Hülshoff family, Haus Hülshoff near Münster – and (below) a bust of the poetess Annette Freiin von Droste-Hülshoff (1797–1841) in the garden.
Opposite: Münster's reconstructed Prinzipalmarkt (marketplace) with the beautifully shaped step gable on the Town Hall and Baroque façades.

Visitors on a guided tour of the city will come across the first of these at the town hall on the Prinzipalmarkt. Although large parts of the historic town centre were destroyed in World War II by fire bombs and explosives, the town hall was authentically restored early on, in the 1950s, since when its elegant Gothic gables have once again presided over the marketplace. It is famous above all for its "Friedenssaal" (peace chamber) under whose splendid wrought iron chandelier delegates came together in 1648 after four years of negotiations to sign a peace document between Spain and the Dutch Republic. Known as the "Peace of Westphalia" it brought Europe one decisive step closer to the ending the Thirty Years' War.
The high-backed stalls on which the delegates sat are original: they were kept in a safe haven during the war and subsequently returned. The local sense of humour manifests itself on cabinet carvings. Somewhat surprisingly in this otherwise dignified ambience they depict men guzzling from jugs, the biblical whale regurgitating Jonah, two monkeys beating one another and two headless men engaged in fisticuffs: possible references to the folly of men and beasts? The three olive-branch-bearing doves depicted on a cast-iron panel by the monumental hearth tell a different story: the inscription reads "Anno 1648. Pax optima rerum, 24 Oct."(Peace is the greatest good).
A city gate once stood opposite the town hall. There is no gate now, just a short road leading into the first formerly walled-in town centre and onto what is now an open space surrounding the cathedral. Founded by Charlemagne, it was the seat of a bishopric established in 791 as an early outpost of mediaeval Christianity dedicated to converting heathens, but also to consolidating the Carolingian-Christian empire. It took some time to complete the process begun by Charlemagne the Great – a process leading in the final instance to the European Union. Building work on

Above: a mighty round-tower of Schloss Diepenbrock near Bocholt. Centre: the Biedermeier-style dining room in the moated castle Haus Hülshoff, home of the Droste-Hülshoff family, to the west of Münster. Below: residence of the Prince Bishop, currently occupied by the University of Münster.
Opposite: Schloss Raesfeld.

the cathedral continued for centuries, and it was the work carried out in the 13th century with the construction of two massive square towers that define its appearance today. The astronomical clock has been marking hours and days since 1542 and is destined to continue its work until the year 2071.
And what about Münster's third historic testament? It is far more ghoulish than the others: high up on the steeple of St Lambert's Church (quite close to the Town Hall) three cages dangle in the air. They were used as showcases for the executed leaders of the Anabaptist rebels who established a "New Jerusalem" in Münster and mustered enough support to resist an 18-month siege by the forces of law and order. The Anabaptists were the fundamentalists of the Reformation. They claimed personal freedom of religion (hence the need for adult baptism) and propagated a kind of early socialist society with conjointly owned community of property independent of state or church control. The rebellion in Münster marked the zenith of their popularity and retribution was dire.

The beauty of moated castles

Living is easy in Münster but the city is almost as famous for its pleasant surroundings: the Münsterland. What makes it so special? For one thing, the wide horizons and the variety of perspectives and panoramas. There is always a little copse or a magnificent single tree to enliven the view over big skies and farmland. Motorists are well advised to follow cyclists onto the smaller roads, crossing a multitude of bridges in various styles and dimensions, or driving alongside any one of the countless streams and water-filled ditches. The farms themselves often nestle in the protective shade of tall trees in happy harmony with their environment. On a slightly larger scale but just as nicely ensconced, the moated castles, for which the Münsterland is justly famous, sit snugly amid the woods.
How many moated castles, palaces and manors are there in the region? One map enumerates a total of 143 in an area stretching from the town of Gütersloh to the Dutch border. Visitors wishing to stay close to Münster will find one of the most beautiful examples about 30 kilometres to the south of the city: the Castle of Vischering near the village of Lüdinghausen, considered by many to be the loveliest of Westphalia's moated structures. Commissioned by a powerful Prince Bishop of Münster, it features a defensive courtyard specially designed to provide extra protection for its aristocratic inhabitants. It is particularly well maintained and is regarded as one of the best examples of a mediaeval fortress castle. Today it functions as a venue for concerts, and the restaurant puts on pageants emulating courtly dinners. Surrounded by woods and a moat, the castle is accessible only via a wooden bridge over the waters in which the old, natural stone walls are beautifully reflected. The three-storeyed semicircular edifice, topped by a tiled gable roof, rises directly from the water on a little island in the middle of the moat. The courtyard opens out towards one side, adorned with beautiful tall trees and a slender tower complete with

Baroque cap: a picture-book romantic castle!
The very old moated Castle of Hülshoff near the village of Havixbeck to the west of Münster is the birthplace of one of Germany's most famous poetesses, Annette von Droste-Hülshoff (1797–1848). Her work is characterised by heightened perception and the great poetic vigour in which she sought comfort from her delicate health and the locally pervasive Catholic conservatism. Following the death of her father, she moved with her mother to Nienberge in the year 1826, to live in the Rüschhaus, a dower-house, part of the family's latifundia. 1838 marked the publication of her first volume of poetry – under a pseudonym, according to her family's wishes. Today, Castle Hülshoff is open to the public. Its furnishings reflect the lifestyle of the local aristocracy during the poetess's lifetime.
The park around the moated castle has been restored according to historical plans. The Rüschhaus dower-house, designed and built by the prominent Westphalian architect Johann Conrad Schlaun, is also open to the public. The living quarters assigned to the poetess in the mezzanine were extremely cramped: she herself referred to them as "a snail's house". She wished to move to the town of Meersburg on Lake Constance, close to her sister and brother-in-law Baron von Lassberg and used the money earned with her first volume of poetry to buy herself property there, the "Prince's Cottage". Some of her most enchanting and atmospheric poetry deals with Westphalian nature and landscape.

UNIQUE ATMOSPHERE

Although it is lies outside the town in pleasant countryside, the Parkhotel Schloss Hohenfelde is easily accessible – with 84 rooms and 12 apartments in the neighbouring Landhaus Hohenfeld, all beautifully appointed and designed to fulfil every wish. In addition to several restaurants, an aperitif bar and "Börneken's" beer parlour, the hotel also features a heated swimming pool, Finnish sauna and solarium, scuba diving courses, bowling alleys and the use of hotel bicycles. Other sporting facilities include tennis and horseback riding.

Parkhotel Schloss Hohenfelde
Dingbänger Weg 400, 48161 Münster
tel.: +49 (0)2534/8080, fax: 7114
www.parkhotel-hohenfeld.de

FOR FURTHER INFORMATION ON MÜNSTER/WESTFALEN

Münster Information
tel.: +49 (0)251/4922710, fax 4927743
websites: www.tourismus.muenster.de, www.muensterland-tourismus.de

Centre: a wealth of mediaeval half-timbered architecture has survived under the gables of this old imperial town. Below: imaginative carvings on today's public library. Opposite: the imperial stronghold was restored in the 19th century, since when it has been the centre point of civic pride in Goslar. Below: audience chamber in the Town Hall.

18 Goslar – "imperial City" in the Harz Region

1000 years of gold and silver

The Harz region boasts many towns with splendid, historic centres. Of these, Goslar is considered the most beautiful, although fans of half timbered structures tend to favour other towns such as Wernigerode, just an hour's drive to the east, and Osterode in the southern Harz. But Goslar offers the visitor a unique combination of history and authentic old town structures. It is also favoured by its situation on the edge of the Harz Mountains, whose foothills rise just beyond the city limits providing a stunning backdrop all year round: green woods and fields, autumn foliage and snow-covered forests.

First-time visitors to the city should enter either from the northeast, through the Breites Tor and the Breite Strasse, or from the southwest, by taking Bergstrasse. All roads lead to the marketplace, with its star-shaped cobblestones and venerable old trees combining to achieve an effect that combines consequence and comfort. The imperial eagle on the market fountain presides proudly over the square and the pointed gables of the late Gothic town hall, the slate – roofed towers of House Kaiserworth, formerly the seat of the Tailors' Guild, and a wonderful variety of half-timbered buildings. The town hall features a magnificent audience chamber with frescoes of emperors and sibyls. Next door, the unequal spires of the market church – one of almost 50 churches and chapels – rise opposite a narrow – fronted house. Formerly known as "Zum Brusttuch", it functions today as a hotel. Its lavish carvings are remarkable above all for the cheekily bare-bottomed butter-maker, locally known as Butterhanne and appreciated as a symbol of down-to-earth, no-nonsense civic vitality. Butterhanne is also credited with the ability to ward off evil spirits. Popular belief has it that witches once rode over the local forests to meet with devils on a mountain called The Brocken (also known as the Blocksberg). As night falls on April 30th, locals and tourists gather and walk up into the hills to celebrate Walpurgis Night around crackling fires. The local arts and crafts

Above: Local atmosphere at the Lohmühle. Centre: Their Imperial Highnesses look down from Kaiserworth House onto the marketplace. Below: Astride their steeds, the emperors pose in front of the Romanesque entrance hall to the Imperial Palace, restored in the 19th century. Opposite: the Imperial Eagle on the market fountain.

industry makes the most of the occasion, producing witches masks, figures of witches riding on brooms and other souvenirs.

How green the pine and plentiful the ore ...

Goslar's oval-shaped and densely built historic town covers barely one square kilometre. So where does all the splendour and wealth come from? Miners dug it out from the depths of the Rammelsberg, a small mountain just beyond the city limits. Archaeologists discovered that metals have been mined here for 3.000 years, long before the city was founded. Tectonic changes, streams of hot lava and intense pressure within the northernmost range of Germany's central mountains created the necessary preconditions: marine sediments were pushed into an incline, strata were "pounded to bits", ores were enriched. The northeast edge of the Harz mountains between Langelsheim and Bad Harzburg, including the area around Goslar, profited from the resulting outcrops and today bears the name of "geology's golden square mile".

A key date in the history of local mining is the year 968 when the Rammelsberg was first mentioned in records. In the Middle Ages, the Ottonian and Salic emperors insisted that mining be continued despite huge risks and harsh conditions. The Rammelsberg yielded above all silver and copper, but also a little gold. Equipped with these riches, Goslar achieved pre-eminence in the northern German Hanseatic league. The 14th and early 15th centuries were times of crisis in the local mining industry, but the following era brought new technologies and greater industrialisation with the result that the production of ore in the Rammelsberg continued until 1988.

At that point it became clear that the huge reserves of nearly 30,000,000 tonnes had been exhausted. However, many of the historic shafts and galleries, man engines and water wheels as well as the surface architecture had been preserved and in 1992, Rammelsberg Mine was made a UNESCO World Heritage Site. Large parts of the mine are open to the public, providing exciting insights into late mediaeval and early modern mining. The man engines are a case in point, consisting of two wooden ladders positioned opposite each another where they rise and fall using the motive power of a water wheel, enabling miners to descend and ascend from the mines by stepping across from one ladder to the other.

Along with the mine, UNESCO also decided to take up Goslar's historic old town and the Kaiserpfalz (Imperial Stronghold) into the illustrious list of World Heritage Sites. 23 Reichstage (Imperial diets) took place in this building following construction in 1050, and German kings and emperors came to Goslar over one hundred times.

The Romanesque building dominates the small hill on which it is set opposite the Domvorhalle (Cathedral narthex), itself a valuable remnant of the cathedral, demolished in 1820. The original Imperial Stronghold was in a sorry state by the 19th century. Today's visitors to what look like ancient stones and old stained-glass windows lining the long imperial assembly hall should bear in mind that these are not original. A kind description would classify the building as a "well-meant" and imaginative restoration, inspired by deep admiration for the Holy Roman Empire of the German Nation. In 1877, a competition was held to find an artist capable of doing justice to be imperial assembly hall. The winner was one Hermann Wislicenus from Thuringia, at that time Professor at the Academy of Fine Arts in Düsseldorf. Along with several of his students, Wislicenus spent 20 years working on the frescoes decorating the hall and they remain a source of delight to aficionados of the Wilhelminian era, which it celebrates in a truly monumental style. Visitors in search of historical accuracy, on the other hand, should turn their attention to an exhibition showing the history of mediaeval "peripatetic imperialism".

Since the 1970s, the town of Goslar has also made a name for itself as a centre of modern art. Tucked away behind a highly decorative façade, the "Mönchehaus Museum", located in a town house dating back to the year 1528, has assembled one of Germany's most impressive municipal art collections, continually supplemented with work by artists from all over the world invited by the town to participate in annual showings and crowned with the presentation of the "Kaiserring" (Imperial ring). Participants in the past have included Henry Moore and Max Ernst, Richard Serra, Christo and Jenny Holzer, whose large-scale sculptures are on view throughout the town. Purchase of these artworks is not financed, as elsewhere, with taxpayers money, but from private funds from the Goslar Association for the Promotion of Modern Art.

In 2010, UNESCO selected the Upper Harz Water Management System for inclusion on its list of World Heritage Sites: Some one hundred lakes (rainwater reservoirs) and over 300 kilometres of ditches combine to make up the world's largest pre-industrial energy supply system.

UNDER STEEP GABLES

The Hotel Zum Brusttuch (Treff Hotel) is situated directly on the marketplace close to the Jakobi Church and derives its name from the many projecting alcoves: a prominent architectural feature. The house is over 475 years old and also famous for the bare bottomed figure of a butter-maker, known as Butterhanne.

Historic restaurant, 13 rooms, swimming pool on the third floor.

Hotel Zum Brusttuch

Hoher Weg 1, 38640 Goslar

tel.: +49 (0)5321/34600, fax: 346099

www.treff-hotels.de

FOR MORE INFORMATION

Goslar Tourismus-Information

tel.: +49 (0)5321/78060, fax: 780644

Websites: www.goslar.de

19 The Gardens of Wörlitz near Dessau

A good idea and well implemented

Every amateur gardener has a dream: a plot of land and free rein to do as one wants, be it trees and shrubs, lakes and streams, or gardens and grottoes. The Alhambra gardens in Granada, the park of Versailles, English landscape gardens or the magically colourful garden created by the artist Niki de Saint-Phalle in Tuscany – all show what can be done with time, space and money.

Centre: the birth of neoclassicism in Germany: Castle Wörlitz near Dessau, constructed since 1766 according to plans drawn up by Friedrich Wilhelm von Erdmannsdorff. Park visitors encounter architectural quotations from various eras, going back to the Middle Ages. The most striking of these is the Gothic house. And bridges everywhere.

One such park is the Dessau-Wörlitz Garden Realm, whose landscaped hills and lawns spread themselves expansively between the meandering waters of the rivers Elbe and Mulde. While Germany was divided, only experts and aficionados knew of this unique park, the creation of an 18th-century German aristocrat. When the wall came down, the state of Sachsen-Anhalt moved quickly to return one of continental Europe's earliest landscape gardens to its original design, complete with several castles and small villages: the "garden realm" in Wörlitz. By the year 2000, restoration work had advanced far enough for UNESCO to give the park its blessing, including it on the list of world Heritage Sites as part of the "Biosphärenreservat Mittlere Elbe" (Middle Elbe Biosphere Reserve). The area alone is impressive, covering 145 square kilometres and welcoming about 2 million visitors a year.

What makes this garden realm so Special?

First and foremost, it is a manifestation of the European Enlightenment: its founder was one of a small group of absolutist nobles blessed with foresight and humanist vision. Duke Leopold III Friedrich Franz von Anhalt-Dessau (1740–1817) was just 18 years of age when he began restructuring his mini-principality, renewing its social life and strengthening its meagre economic forces. He looked above all to England for his models, with special emphasis on farming, industry and lifestyle. His motto, based on that of the Roman poet Horace, was: "The beautiful should be useful and the useful beautiful." In practical terms this meant that his gardens were not created solely for representational purposes, but also fulfilled ecological and economic criteria.
The young Duke of Dessau was warmly praised for his efforts by the most influ-

Above and right: There is some architectural rarity hidden behind every group of trees. Centre: the historic kitchen buildings serve snacks and beverages. Opposite: peacocks have been popular ornaments in the gardens of European nobility ever since ancient Rome – seen here in front of the Gothic House.

ential personages of the day: King Frederick II of Prussia (Frederick the Great), Johann Joachim Winckelmann, who 'rediscovered' Greek antiquity, Johann Caspar Lavater of Switzerland, the poet Goethe, and the great natural historian Alexander von Humboldt.

In the 18th century, before the canalisation of rivers, there was far more wilderness than today and many travellers regarded the man-made landscape around Dessau und Wörlitz as "the most beautiful countryside in the realm". Softly rising hills and undulating lawns spread over wide horizons: paths, trees and copses, lakes and canals, ornate castle façades and farm buildings all found an appropriate setting. Today, all this appears less extraordinary than it did 200 years ago. If anything, visitors are surprised by the reticence and consideration exercised in restructuring a natural environment. The peaceful aura and uplifting views, enhanced by strategically placed monuments and exemplary works of art, are a delight to behold. The Culture Foundation Dessau Wörlitz and Wörlitz Information Office are happy to delineate suitable itineraries, depending on the time available. You can wander round the entire garden or concentrate on the historical centre. Non-motorized travellers should take a local train from Dessau to Wörlitz via Oranienbaum: a thirty-minute ride. It is only a couple of minutes from the station into the heart of the park and to the castle situated on the lake. Does the wide façade and columned portico remind you of another, world-famous building? The White House in Washington is definitely bigger but, like Castle

Wörlitz, it was built in the style of an English country manor, modelled upon designs by the great Renaissance architect Andrea Palladio. In this case the architect was Baron Friedrich Wilhelm von Erdmannsdorff (1736–1800), close friend of the Duke and local ruler Franz, with whom he had travelled extensively throughout England and Italy.

After leaving the castle, it's time to tackle the grounds, which are divided into five different types of garden: the Temple of the Goddesses Flora and Venus, for example, or the Palm House and the summer rooms, the sandstone sarcophagus inscribed with verses by the German poet Klopstock and evidence of the Duke's religious tolerance in the form of a synagogue, severely damaged in 1938 but preserved nonetheless thanks to the efforts of a courageous garden director. The Duke was very partial to the modern Italian – English neoclassical style popular at the time, but also promoted

the eminently German neo-Gothic style. One splendid example is the beautifully restored "Gothic House" with its emphatic, highlighted Gothic ogees – based in this case on Tudor Gothic, a Venetian church, and the historic town hall of Breslau.

More?

There is, in fact, much more to discover: the quirky and the beautiful – alongside many references to the Enlightenment and its educative zeal. The 17 bridges spanning the streams and canals all demonstrate various aspects of bridge building, for example, although none of them actually provide access to the Rousseau island, for which the Duke commissioned a copy of the great French philosopher's grave, surrounded by tall poplars.

"Gardeners, artists, philosophers, poets – go to Wörlitz!" Solid advice, as given by the Duke of Ligne, himself a creator of gardens. Others referred to a Garden of Eden. It has even been called a "Museum of World Culture". Throughout almost 60 years of governance, Duke Franz extended the overall dimensions of his realm to include the neighbouring areas around Oranienbaum Palace, Sieglitzer Forest and Park and the Luisium Manor. He founded a school, was the first local ruler to introduce mandatory cowpox vaccinations, and instigated widespread agricultural reform. Today, Duke Franz's garden realm is a natural and integral part of the Middle Elbe Biosphere Reserve and a shining example of the harmonious and mutually fruitful interplay of nature and civilisation.

UNDER THE OLD LIME TREES

The country Hotel Wörlitzer Hof is situated directly on the periphery of the garden realm with 47 rooms available either in standard or comfort class, in addition to a family apartment and two wedding suites.
Landhaus Wörlitzer Hof
Markt 96, 06786 Wörlitz
tel. +49 (0)34905/4110, fax: 41122
www.woerlitzer-hof.de
handicapped facilities

FOR MORE INFORMATION ON THE WÖRLITZER GARTEN REALM AND DESSAU

Kulturstiftung Dessau Wörlitz
tel.: +49 (0)34905/4090, fax: 40930
Websites: www.ksdw.de, www.gartenreich.de, www.zerbst.anhalt.de, www.woerlitz-information.de
Like the Wörlitz Park, the Bauhaus centre and adjoining buildings are also on the UNESCO list of World Heritage Sites. In 1925, Walter Gropius designed the Bauhaus School (restored 1975/76), until 1932 it was a centre for architecture and graphic art.
www.welterbestaetten.de/de/dessau.htm

20 Ivy-lined Legend around the Wartburg

Singers, a saint and the "Knight George"

Nothing engaged the Romantic imagination more than legends involving knights and the feudal life of mediaeval castles. The beautifully situated Wartburg is uniquely linked to prominent personalities of the time. Its name has become synonymous with local legend, frequently invoked by artists and musicians. Ludwig Bechstein (1801–1860), a collector of legend and fable, called the Wartburg the "northern star of Thuringian history, on whose walls, crenels and crevices the green ivy of legend decoratively clings."

Romantic views over the forests of Thuringia from a romantic castle. Opposite: a castle dating back to the 12th century, complete with additions: seen here, the Great Hall, the Bailey, Knight's House and Bailiwick. Opposite below: a glimpse into an exhibition of rare artefacts, and into Martin Luther's modest workplace.

The young Richard Wagner found material here on which to base his opera *Tannhäuser*: a collection of local myth and legend in which Bechstein first brought together the figure of Tannhauser, Castle Wartburg and the enchanted Hörselberg mountain, in which Venus, the pagan goddess of love, holds court.

Wagner knew the Wartburg, and was, in fact, reminded of the castle whilst walking through the forests of Bohemia around Schreckenstein Castle whilst he was working on *Tannhäuser*. This was to be the first of his operas in which music itself was thematically relevant – in the singing contest, for example, as well as in the role played by church bells. He also modified the historical figures of Tannhäuser and St Elizabeth so that Tannhäuser became credible as a man, caught between earthly and celestial love. The opera's Dresden première in October of 1845, staged in the Royal Court Theatre of Saxony, was not successful but the following performances aroused more enthusiasm.

"In many respects, the ideal castle"

We know that legends are not fairy tales: they are too close to history. Tannhäuser was an historical figure, a contemporary of St Elizabeth known as "tanhusaere" in the crusade led by Emperor Frederick II. A visit to Castle Wartburg puts this history in context only a short walk from the town of Eisenach. In winter, the Castle is visible through the bare branches of trees dotting the gardens of Eisenach's villas. Yet walking to the castle takes one into the

The head of Christ

The castle courtyard and monument of Martin Luther in Eisenach, where the church reformer's sojourn in Eisenach and on the Wartburg is also commemorated in the "Luther House" memorial site. Opposite: the gate and Church of St Nicholas in Eisenach.

woods on the edge of the Thüringer Wald Nature Reserve, which stretches all the way to Franconia and covers over 2000 square kilometres. It's best to arrive early, before tourists arrive to fill the chambers and courtyards.

In 1999, the World Heritage Committee declared the Wartburg a World Heritage Site, calling it "in many respects, the ideal castle". Approaching the castle after a final steep ascent and entering the premises through high, imposing walls, visitors will find themselves surrounded by nearly 1000 years of history now restored to shining splendour. Generations of restorers have worked here, recreating this mediaeval structure with cobblestones and seasoned timber.

When Goethe spent some weeks here in 1777 as Privy Counsellor for the Duchy of Saxe – Weimar, he found the castle in a state of disrepair. The Duke provided rooms in the Knights' House and Goethe was delighted, writing to Frau von Stein that: "these rooms are simply wonderful, so high, so liberating that I'd rather not stay too long for fear that height and happiness should prove too much". Goethe kept a sketchbook and his drawings were consulted as important documents when it came to restoring the castle. In fact, the celebrated writer was an early advocate of the castle's restoration, proposing the foundation of a museum for old German art as early as 1815. However, it was only in 1838, some years after Goethe's death, that Grand Duke Carl Alexander commissioned Hugo von Ritgen, an architect from Giessen, with the castle's restoration. Ritgen devoted a large part of his career to this task, although he did not always respect historical authenticity, preferring to work in the spirit of romantic historicism.

Luther outlawed

There are two different histories on view today at the Wartburg: on the one hand, its mediaeval origins, on the other, nearly 200 years of restoration work. Construction work on the castle began in the 11th century but large parts of this structure burned down in 1317, after which a new south tower was added. The high-ceilinged room in which Martin Luther took refuge after the Diet of Worms declared him outlawed (to be killed without legal consequence) is as barely furnished now as it was then. It was in this room that Luther, as "Knight George" under the protection of the Prince Elector of Saxe, Frederick the Wise, took just 11 weeks to translate the New Testament from Greek to German: an inestimable contribution to the dissemination of standard German as a spoken and written language. Nonetheless, the months spent at Wartburg were difficult for Luther and plagued by illness. Letters kept him informed of religious and political developments and allowed him to exercise influence himself, but the scope of his activity was limited and in 1522 he risked the return to Wittenberg.

In contrast to Luther's Room, the Great Hall, which is probably one of the oldest rooms in the castle, bears little resemblance to its original appearance. Although the beamed ceiling and mediaeval stone columns speak one language, they are contradicted by the frescoes painted in 1854 by Moritz von

Schwind in a distinctly 19th-century idiom. The same applies to the Hall of Minstrels. Elizabeth's chamber commemorates the Hungarian princess who married Landgrave Ludwig IV in 1221 and lived here in emulation of St Francis of Assisi in poverty, devoting her life to the poor. The opulent frescoes in the chamber were painted in the early 20th century – a gift from Emperor William II. The presence of so many different eras has the advantage of bringing together very different aspects of German history, music and art under one prominent roof. The Wartburg Festival, first held in 1817 by 500 students calling for German unity, was an early intimation of the castle's future role as a symbol of German history, confirmed once and for all in 1990, the first year of reunification, when a grand total of 776,000 visitors " stormed" the Wartburg.

Those wishing to explore properly the woods to the south of the Wartburg (as opposed to just enjoying the view from the castle), will enjoy the walk to Wilhelmsthal Castle. The designated footpath stays fairly close to Route 19 as it winds its way through the rocky Dragon's Gorge. A parallel footpath further west takes ramblers through high forests along the Werra-Burgen-Steig path or the Rennsteig path, to the spot where they meet at the rustically appointed Hohen Sonne Inn. Either one of two more footpaths lead go on to Wilhelmsthal Castle, which dates from the early 18th century and features a rowing pond and stone garden vases. A plan conceived by the celebrated landscape artist Prince Pückler-Muskau to create a landscaped park from Wilhelmsthal to the Wartburg was never realized: it was simply too ambitious.

RENOVATED VILLA, SMART DESIGN

The Hotel Villa Anna is situated in pleasantly quiet grounds in Eisenach's Villa district not far from the Prinzenteich and within walking distance to the Wartburg. The hotel has been carefully renovated and now features a smart, modern design.

Hotel Villa Anna
Fritz-Koch-Strasse 12, 99817 Eisenach
tel.: +49n(0)3691/23950, Fax 239530
www.hotel-villa-anna.de

FOR MORE INFORMATION ON THE WARTBURG

tel.: +49 (0)3691/79230, fax: 792320
Websites: www.eisenach.de, www.schaetze-der-welt.de, www.wartburg-eisenach.de, www.burgenperlen.de, www.deutsche-burgen.org, www.luther.de

The home of Weimar Classicism on the River Ilm, attentively restored. Centre: Stone bridge near the castle. Below: an ideal of friendship, chiselled in stone: Goethe and Schiller in front of the theatre. Opposite: Goethe's residence during the early Weimar years, the Garden House in the Ilm park. Opposites, below: young ladies and old classics.

21 Weimar, Goethe, World Culture

A green and fertile valley on the Ilm

The 63,000 inhabitants of Weimar are spoiled for choice when it comes to museums and castles, poets' houses and monuments – as well as an immensely valuable library, which only just survived a fire in 2004 and is now in the process of reconstruction. The poetry and wisdom of the movement called Weimar Classicism originated here. No less than twelve of these localities (including four parks) have been declared World Heritage Sites by UNESCO.

Part of the city's beauty and charm resides in a modest little river linking some of these sites. Generations of locals and city councillors deserve praised for foiling plans to despoil this picturesque little valley with speculative projects. Visitors to Weimar can walk along the river into a town in which time seems to have stood still since 1800.

A young duke and his friend from Frankfurt

Cultural life in the Weimar of 1760, capital of the Duchy of Saxe-Weimar with 6,000 inhabitants, is dominated by a young widow: Anna-Amalia, born in 1739 as a Princess of Brunswick-Wolfenbüttel, married the Duke of Weimar, and was widowed by the age of 20. As regent, she gathered around her intellectual giants such as Christoph Martin Wieland, ensuring that the city gained a reputation as a centre of European culture 250 years before UNESCO confirmed the status.

In 1775, Anna-Amalia's son Carl August took over the regency. He travelled first to Darmstadt, where he married Luise, Princess of Hesse-Darmstadt, stopping on the return journey in Frankfurt to renew his acquaintance with the poet Goethe, nine years older than the Duke. A friendship developed between the two young men. As author of "The Sorrows of Young Werther" and the drama "Götz von Berlichingen", Goethe had already achieved a measure of fame. Carl August said of Goethe that: "he talks a lot, but eloquently and originally, naïvely even – and is startlingly amusing and funny." Carl August invited Goethe to stay at court. The poet hesitated before agreeing, despite his father's reservations. There was a misunderstanding, Goethe was on the point of departing for Italy but then, after a four day trip by carriage, he arrived in

Schiller
Der Geisterseher

Goethe
Schiller
Balladen
ECKERMANNS
GESPRÄCHE MIT
GOETHE

Views of Weimar, above: in the Ilm park, centre: entrance to the town hall, below: taking tourists for a ride around the Frauenplan. Opposite: in the Goethe House on the Frauenplan, gift from the Duke to his famous friend to accommodate books, mineral specimens, paintings, sculptures, manuscripts. Opposite, outside right: the Bauhaus Museum.

UNESCO Sites
World Cultural Heritage in Weimar:

The Princes' Tomb and Historic Cemetery – Goethe's House – Schiller's House – City Castle – The Duchess Anna Amalia Library – City Church of Sts Peter and Paul – Herder House – Old High School – Goethe's Garden and Goethe's Garden House – Park on the Ilm with the Roman House – Belvedere Castle, Orangery and Park – Tiefurt Castle and Park – Ettersburg Castle and Park – Wieland Manor and Park

Weimar with his servant Philipp Seidel and a courtier on November 7th, 1775, at five o'clock in the morning.
Six months later, the young Duke presented his friend and adviser with a gift: a garden house in the Ilm valley. It was an unofficial present: the contract specified Goethe as the buyer of garden and garden house "including all its non-removable contents." The poet lived here for six years with his servant, and returned here again and again in later years from his house on the Frauenplan. Coming from town across the Sternbrücke bridge by the Town Palace, guests walk through the well-tended park on the River Ilm and imagine the rampant greenery surrounding the house when Goethe lived here – or should one say found refuge here? The poet was an assiduous companion to the young Duke but found life at court stifling and sought respite in nature. The Duke's gift was a good choice.
The Duke intended to modernise and reform all aspects of life in the Duchy, and was ably supported by Goethe, who was more than happy to invest his energies in "some years of useful employment, better by far than the idle life back home", where his work as a lawyer bored him. By June 1776, he had advanced to become one of the four members of the Privy Council, was entitled to call himself legation councillor and soon exercised the functions of minister responsible for mining, forestry and agriculture and also for the military, which he cut back to save money. Yet he still found time to tend the fruit trees in his garden and lay out a landscaped park in the Ilm Valley, a project jointly undertaken with Duke Carl August and based on the park in Wörlitz, newly created by the young Duke Franz von Anhalt-Dessau.

Memories of happiness and love

Several of the garden monuments in the park date from the poet's tenure. In the year 1777 he set out "the stone of good fortune" in his garden, with an inscription ending in the words: "stay here and bring me fortune, through you alone shall I speak. Like the Muse alighting upon the chosen one, kissing him amiably on the lips." It was also Goethe's idea to set up the Snake's Stone, not as a reminder of original sin, but as a sign of protection and help, like the snake on the staff of the Greek God of medicine and healing, Asclepius.
Then there is the stairway set into rocks above the small bridge crossing the Ilm,

created in memory of a young lady, Christel von Lasswitz, jilted by her lover and found drowned in the Ilm clutching a copy of Goethe's "The Sarrows of Young Werther". This small flight of stairs also provided the quickest access to the apartments inhabited by Frau von Stein (the poet once walked to her summer residence outside town on the Kochberg, reminding her in one of his letters that it took him four hours to get there).

Four weeks after his return from Italy and disappointed by his reunion with Frau von Stein, Goethe met Christiane Vulpius. Their relationship began here, in the Garden House, and lasted for one third of the poet's life, from 1788 to Christiane's death in 1816. For much of this time, court society looked down upon the poet's partner, considering her socially inferior, only sanctioning his choice late in the day. The Duke, however, stood by his friend and even agreed to be godfather to August, Goethe's firstborn son.

The network of sites and relationships extends outwards from the garden house through the Ilm Valley and further on to the modest, manorial Castle Tiefur, where Carl August's mother Anna Amalia spent the summer months. In the other direction, the river flows past the villages of Oberweimar and Ehringdorf and on, via Belvedere Alley, to the ducal Belvedere Palace.

PURE ROMANTICISM

Located on the city outskirts in the direction of Schöndorf, surrounded by fields, the Hotel Dorotheenhof, formerly a manor house belonging to cavalry captain Carl von Kalckreuth, today's "Romantik Hotel" has 60 comfortably appointed rooms, a vaulted ceiling in the restaurant and good cuisine. The "Schöndorf-Suite" has its own sauna.

Dorotheenhof

Dorotheenhof 1, 99427 Weimar
tel.: +49 (0)3643/459-0, fax: 459-200
www.dorotheenhof.com

FOR FURTHER INFORMATION ON WEIMAR

Tourist Information Weimar

tel.: +49 (0)3643/7450, fax: 459-200
Websites: www.weimar.de, www.weimar-klassik.de, www.naturparkreisen.de

22 Hiking with Goethe to Dornburg Castles in the Saale Valley

"The view is magnificent and cheering"

Long walks were popular in Goethe's day, a chance to immerse oneself in nature. One fine day in July of 1777, a group of young men set out into the Saale Valley: Duke Carl August of Weimar, his brother, Vice Regent of Mainz, the 28-year-old poet Goethe, his friend Knebel and the Einsiedel brothers. They clambered up and down the rocks at Kunitzburg Castle and walked through the pouring rain back to the Dornburg castles, spending the night on straw pallets – not exactly lordly, but good enough.

Sitting atop their 100 metre-high rocky outcrop, the Dornburg castles were long threatened with decay but have now been restored, above all, the Rococo castle (above and opposite) and the Renaissance castle (below) in which visitors may experience the kind of atmosphere enjoyed by Goethe in 1828.

There are three castles on the range of hills overlooking the River Saale near Dornburg: the Old Castle, a Renaissance castle and a Rococo castle. Nothing has remained of the earlier Ottonian fort except the lower section of the castle tower. Documents – the oldest signed by Poppo, Chancellor to Otto I., in 937 – testify to Dornburg's role as an Imperial fortress, stopover and residence for many German rulers in the 10th and 11th centuries. It was only around 1500 that the " Old Castle" was built, later to be used as a dowager house by Anna Maria, Duchess of Weimar. The attractive Renaissance castle, originally built by a member of the landed aristocracy, passed through several hands before being purchased in 1824 by Grand Duke Carl August. This is where the almost 80-year-old Goethe sought refuge for several months in 1828 after he had organised the burial of his friend Carl August, who died on June 14th. Following German reunification, the

Ether, in the clouds it bears,
Quarrels with the candid day,
And east wind, for the sun, prepares
A blue path, chasing them away.
With pure heart thank the mild great one,
With moving gaze the scene behold,
Then will the reddish setting sun
Ring the horizon round with gold.

Johann Wolfgang von Goethe (1828)
Translation: Christopher Middleton

Renaissance castle was carefully and completely restored, whilst only the interior of the Rococo castle was renovated. The Old Castle also received a general overhaul and is now used by the University of Jena. Stop for a meal on the narrow terrace fronting the Renaissance castle or stay the night (if you don't mind sharing bathrooms).

Rambling with Goethe

To follow Goethe's footsteps, arrive in the afternoon leaving time to view the castles and in particular, the poet's rooms. If you come by train, make your own way up from the valley on pleasant and well signposted paths. Next day, this path will take you down, across the railway line and southwards through the village of Dornburg. Cockerels crow as one leaves behind the cottage gardens with their hollyhocks and sunflowers. A series of blue/white markings will take you upwards on quiet paths, from which there are views of the castles and the tree-lined river below. It can get hot up here but there is always a group of trees ahead to provide some shade. Don't forget to keep an eye on the markings and look out for the specially signposted picnic areas, followed further on by a monument for the fallen of World War I: "Into our games/burst the war ...".

The "Gasthof zum Gleistal" welcomes walkers for lunch, and then it's time to descend into the valley through fields and apple trees. Buzzards – and sometimes model aeroplanes – circle the skies above the walls of Castle Kunitzburg. Through the window niches in the ruins of the Great Hall one can look down on to Kunitz and further, towards Jena. The Imperial fortress was already a ruin in 1500. If you're lucky, you'll be served refreshments today by the "Friends of Kunitzburg". Intrepid walkers can press on to the city of Jena. The less enthusiastic might want to take the tram from Zwätzen.

To veils of mist in morning light
Disclosed are garden, valley, hill,
And cups of flowers with colours bright
To the most ardent longing fill.

IN GOETHE'S FOOTSTEPS

The Renaissance Castle, in which Goethe lived, has a few simply appointed rooms in the upper floor with wonderful views but no en-suite bathrooms. Breakfast is provided. The restaurant specialises in local Thuringian cuisine, coffee and cake in the castle café, tour through the historical castle gardens with musical accompaniment.
tel.: and fax +49 (0)36427/70419
(Margit Scheffel + Harald Janotta. Markt 26, 07778 Dornburg)

FOR FURTHER INFORMATION ON DORNBURG CASTLES

Dornburg Tourist
tel.: +49 (0)36427/20934, fax: 75598
Jena Tourist Information
tel.: +49 (0)3641/4980
Websites: www.jena.de, www.jena.de/tourism/deutsch/dornburg.htm,
www.dornburger-schloesser.de/geschichte
The castles are closed from November to the end of April.

23 Dresden's Panorama of the River Elbe – Past and Present

Illustrious art-lovers: Prince Electors and Kings

The energy and enterprise of the local populace can be a powerful force, as evidenced by the return of the Baroque cupola on top of Dresden's Frauenkirche (Church of our Lady), resplendently restored to its rightful place in the city's silhouette. In 1991, soon after German reunification, a citizens' action group was founded to support the reconstruction of the largest Baroque Protestant parish church in Germany. For decades, the site had been nothing more than a huge heap of rubble, a reminder of the bombing raid carried out on a city overflowing with refugees.

Centre: generous donations enabled the reconstruction of the Frauenkirche and restoration of the city silhouette.
Below: the cigarette factory Yenidze adds an oriental touch to Dresden's largely Baroque architecture. Opposite: in front of the Saxon Academy of Arts: the architect Gottfried Semper.

Half a century after the terrible night of the 13th – 14th February 1945, the people of Dresden set about picking out one building stone after another from the ruins, categorising them, when possible, based on their original placement, and labelling them: a procedure that remains historically unique. Thousands of people from all around the world helped and continue to help the people of Dresden with generous donations. Some of many recent highlights: after initially failing to properly recast the bells, the second successful attempt in April 2003 culminated in a ringing-in of the seven new bells on June 7th in the presence of 40,000 onlookers. In April 2004, the last of over one million stones was set, the church finally complete. In June of 2004, the 28-ton copper orb was lifted into place on top of the cupola drum. Since February 1st, 2005, visitors can enjoy the view from an observation platform onto "Florence on the Elbe", and in the very same month, the reconstructed Church of our Lady was taken up into the international Community of the Cross of Nails: the Cathedral Chaplain of Coventry presented the city of Dresden with a cross made with nails gathered from the debris of his own cathedral following the German bombing raids of 1940–41 as a sign of reconciliation. In September 2005, the people of Dresden celebrated the re-consecration of their church. The use of historical building substance means that the

GOTTFRIED
SEMPER

Above: single horsepower in front of the court church. Centre: detail of the princely procession painted onto 25,000 porcelain tiles (1875). Below: excursion on the River Elbe. Opposite: the famous Semper Opera, formerly the Royal Court Theatre, built by Gottfried Semper 1838–41. Opposite right: the cupola on the newly restored Frauenkirche.

church's history – its destruction and reconstruction – remains visible. The destiny of this building, its place in the hearts and minds of the people of Dresden, is literally set in stone.

Dresden – The growth of beauty

No doubt the river's gracious lines play a role. When the Elbe flows majestically into Dresden from the East, tracing a double curve from left to right to left and right again, it does so with a generosity more than capable of inspiring architects (on the map, the river looks a little like a loosely written M). In Dresden, the first river curve is home to the Brühl Terraces, named after Prime Minister Heinrich Graf von Brühl, himself a collector of art, who unapologetically championed the purchase of art from all over Europe by the Prince Electors of Saxe, King Augustus III and his predecessor Augustus the Strong so as to "blind the foreign emissaries and other illustrious strangers with the bright lights emanating from the court of Saxe."

Dresden indeed accomplished an almost meteoric rise in the first half of the 18th century, when it occupied the position of "premier city of arts in the North" (according to the art historian Johann Joachim Winckelmann). The first 100 years after the Wettin dynasty moved its court from the old residence in Meissen to the new residence Dresden (1485) had been a time of expansive construction: city walls, Castle and the Jägerhof (hunting lodge). There followed great hardship: the Thirty Years' War and post-war distress. When Augustus the Strong (Augustus II, who governed 1694–1733) inherited the throne, Europe watched in astonishment as he went about transforming his residence into a European metropolis.

Even in the context of the splendid Baroque era, a building such as the Dresdner Zwinger stands out as unique. It wasn't all down to the monarchs: let's not forget the architects who carried out Augustus the Strong's ideas. First and foremost of these is the Westphalian Matthäus Daniel Pöppelmann, summoned to the Court of Saxony in 1686, before the reign of Augustus. The state of Saxony owes him a debt of gratitude for buildings such as the Zwinger, the redesign of the Japanese Palace (or Porcelain Palace) and the palaces at Pillnitz and Großsedlitz, not forgetting his mature work: the Augustus Bridge. In Warsaw (the Prince Electors of Saxeony, Augustus II and III, were also Kings of Poland) Pöppelmann built the Royal Palace and the Saxon Palace.

Pöppelmann was generous in his use of ornamentation and building. And yet most of his buildings, which mark the transition from Baroque to Rococo are characterised by a definitive elegance, solidly built, but without overburdened gravitas. Augustus the Strong called upon the services of other architects, including the Frenchmen Zacharias Longuelune and Jean de Bodt, as well as Georg Bähr from the Erz Mountains. Known for his church buildings, Bähr was the architect behind Dresden's Frauenkirche (1726–33) with its oval central space, surrounded by seven levels of galleries. It was his idea to construct the cupola vaulting using only stone.

Abundance of painting and music

Dresden can never achieve the integrity of its pre-war appearance, no matter how much energy and care is invested in the restoration of its representational buildings. However, the correlation between the River Elbe and the structures comprising the town centre is slowly being re-established through the refurbishment of elements such as the Carola Bridge and Mary Bridge, the Brühl Gardens and the small lake by the Zwinger, coming closer, step-by-step, to the architectural ensemble painted so lucidly by Bernardo Belotto, (Canaletto) in the 18th century.

There were further contributions to come in the 19th century above all, those designed by Hamburg-born Gottfried Semper (1803–79), who advocated a return to the clear forms of the Renaissance. From 1834–49, Semper taught and worked in Dresden, building first the court theatre, known as the Semper Opera, then the synagogue and finally the Semper Gallery. The museums in Dresden are full of major European works of art, which also benefited from efforts of courageous helpers on several occasions – notably at the end of World War II and during the floods of 2002. The prosperity that came with 19th-century industrialisation led to the development of wealthy residential districts (Loschwitz, Blasewitz, Weißer Hirsch). In the early 20th century, the Munich-based architect Richard Riemerschmid built the garden city of Hellerau, demonstrating a lighter approach to residential living. The hilly countryside around Dresden between Saxon Switzerland and Meissen has a beauty of its own, evident in the pleasant suburbs that spread on the slopes above the River Elbe, home once again to the old panorama boats and historical ships.

QUIET AND CENTRAL

Just a few minutes away from strikingly designed "Blue Wonder" bridge, in one of Dresden's most agreeable districts, the hotel Hotel Am Blauen Wunder offers its visitors quiet rooms and Italian cuisine and in the "Culinario" restaurant. Rental bikes provide easy access to the historic town centre via the bicycle path along the Elbe.
Hotel Am Blauen Wunder
Lockwitzer Strasse 48, 01309 Dresden
tel.: +49 (0)351/33660, fax: 3366299
www.hotelamblauenwunder.de

FOR MORE INFORMATION ON DRESDEN

tel.: +49 (0)351/49192100, fax: 49192116
Websites:
www.dresden.de,
www.dresden-tourist.de,
www.frauenkirche-dresden.com,
www.wiederaufbau-Frauenkirche.de

24 National Park Saxon Switzerland – and more

Centre: the Kirnitzschtalbahn tram takes visitors to the Lichtenhainer waterfalls. Below: taking a break between rock towers. Opposite: an evening view from the Bastei rocks over the Elbe valley. Opposite right: this column in the Elb Sandstone Mountains bears a hero's name: "the great column of Hercules". Opposite below: Königstein fortress.

Unexpected: Rock-climbing in Saxony

Why are there so many excellent rock climbers in Saxony? Because the best place to practise rock-climbing is right outside Dresden itself. Otherwise known as the Elbe Sandstone Mountains, the bizarrely formed rock towers are accessible via 1200 km of trails leading through cool and moist green valleys. There are no less than 1600 via ferrata (assisted mountaineering trails) on the rock towers themselves, affording bird's eye views of the Elbe from vantage points such as the Basteifelsen at an altitude of 200 metres.

The National Park, founded in 1990, comprises only 93 square kilometres – supplemented however by 275 square kilometres of protected landscape. The smaller part of the national park extends to the west of Bad Schandau, the larger part to the east from Bad Schandau to the Czech border where the Schrammstein rocks raise their three fingers. Nature lovers will find rare plants and animals: the lynx, the black stork and some varieties of owl, if they are lucky.
Geologically speaking, the Elbe Sandstone Mountains originated in the cretaceous age, under water. For millions of years, layers of sand and clay fossilized. Following a vast upheaval, the ocean drained off, leaving behind a 600-metre-deep layer of sandstone, and the River Elbe began the process of erosion, working away at countless gullies, crevices and gorges to create the landscape of towers and tabletop mountains referred to from the 19th century onwards as "Saxon Switzerland". On the other side of the border, the continuation of this landscape is called "Bohemian Switzerland".

An excursion to Upper Lusatia: Castle Stolpen

In addition to sandstone, granite and basalt also occur in Saxon Switzerland. The most interesting basalt formations, however, are located to the northwest of the little town of Stolpen. The name derives from the Sorbian "Stolpy", meaning "columns." The formations are called the "Stolpen organ pipes." Both designations refer to the basalt structures and their astonishingly even,

densely positioned polygonal columns. Castle Stolpen was built on one such dark red, brownish basalt tip.
At the castle, the guide recounts an interesting story about one Countess Anna Constanze Cosel (1680–1765), incarcerated within the castle walls for almost 50 years. Why? As a young woman, she was the mistress of Augustus the Strong, whom she once dared to criticise – reason enough to have her imprisoned for life.
Königstein Fortress is situated a little closer to the national park. Originally part of Bohemia, it was taken over by the House of Wettin in the mid-15th century. The Saxon Prince Electors and kings used the fortress to store both their treasures and prominent prisoners. An alchemist and porcelain maker named Böttger rather recklessly exchanged letters with interested parties in Berlin on the secret of porcelain making and found himself spending time here – as did the Russian anarchist Bakunin, the Social Democrat Bebel and the poet Wedekind.
Bad Schandau's sights are less morbid: the town is known above all as a spa and also as the site of Renaissance buildings including the old Brewery and the old Town Hall with its crests and coats of arms. The Renaissance altar created around 1575 with sandstone and semi-precious stones by Hans Walther was originally intended for a church in Dresden, but found its way instead to Bad Schandau in 1927. Fans of the great outdoors should consider a trip on the Kirnitzschtalbahn tram, which has taken visitors up to the Lichtenhainer waterfalls since 1898.

WELL LOCATED

The Hotel Ostrauer Scheibe is centrally located in Bad Schandau.
Hotel Ostrauer Scheibe
Alter Schulweg 12, 01814 Bad Schandau-Ostrau (going towards Smilka)
tel.+49 (0)35022/4880, fax: 48888
info@ostrauer-scheibe.de

FOR MORE INFORMATION ON THE ELB SANDSTONE MOUNTAINS

Tourismusverband Sächsische Schweiz
tel.: +49 (0)35022/4950, fax: 49533
Bad Schandau – Haus des Gastes
tel.: +49 (0)35022/90030, fax: 90034
Websites: www.saechsische-schweiz.de

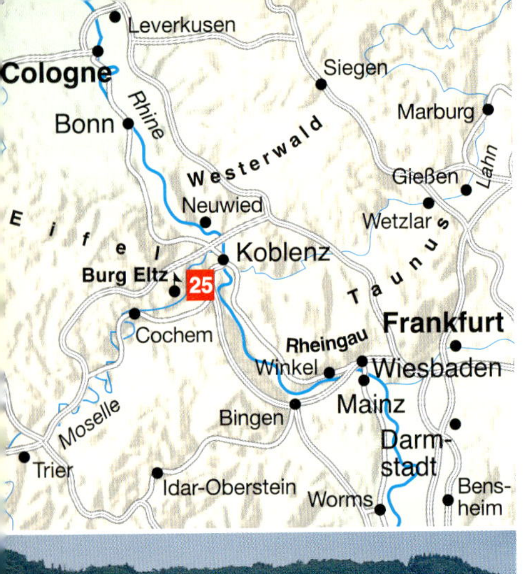

25 The Moselle Valley and Castle Eltz

Vineyards and other cultural treasures

The River Moselle is intrinsically European, with its origins in France and Luxembourg and an old, Roman history. Its well-defined meanders weave their way through the Rhenish Slate Uplands, doubling the distance from Trier to Koblenz as the crow flies. The last curve is drawn around the town of Cochem, one of the busiest on the Moselle with 1.5 million day-trippers a year. Nonetheless, the town maintains its friendly atmosphere.

Centre: riverboats on the Moselle – as charter services or round trips, under mostly steep vineyards. Below: the stately Town Hall of Cochem, near the meander known as "Cochemer Krampen". Opposite: close-up onto Castle Eltz, nestling on its rocky outcrop, surrounded by green forest.

One reason might be the protection afforded by a steep mountain and mountaintop castle, the Reichsburg. However, the castle is not a mediaeval relic but more of a 19th century bauble created for a railway industrialist from Berlin who loved castles and had this one built on the ruins of an earlier castle destroyed in the year 1689 by General Vauban (fighting for Louis XIV). Today, the castle belongs to the town and houses a museum. With its narrow, climbing alleys, gates, crenels and half timbered structures, Cochem is one of the most attractive towns on the Moselle. The list of local wines reads like a Who's Who of viticulture, with names of great poetic resonance: Ürziger Würzgarten, Erdener Treppchen, Piesporter Goldtröpfchen, Trittenheimer Altärchen, Bernkasteler Doktor, Longuicher (from Longus vicus, = long village) Herrenberg,. Only the town of Kröv has given its wine an un-poetically sober name.

Mosel wines owe their superb quality to the slate-based soil, steep slopes which catch maximum sunlight, and the warmth-reflecting river. The fine Riesling wines, pressed from grapes harvested under great effort from steep slopes have their price (flatter and easily accessible vineyards are used to cultivate the Müller-Thurgau grape, and the upper Moselle area is home to a very old grape known as Elbling). People come to the Moselle to enjoy landscapes alternating between hill and valley. They come by boat or bicycle to enjoy not just the wine but beautiful towns and cultural traditions.

Upriver from Cochem, for example, the village of Beilstein is so picturesquely situated that it has often been used in films and TV series. It faces the Bremmer Kalmont on the other side of the river – the steepest vineyard in the area where grape pickers need a good head for heights. Some miles upstream, the town

Above: Riesling wines from the Moselle, formerly considered too sweet, now famous for their well-tuned flavours. Centre: another view of Cochem, where a four-kilometre train tunnel takes goods and passengers under the town and the vineyards. Opposite above: summer life in front of Cochem's Town Hall. Opposite below: Cochem in the evening light.

of Traben-Trarbach sits snugly on both sides of the river (in the 19th century, Prussian authorities insisted on merging the two competing wine villages to form a double – town). Today, an interesting local history museum is located in the former Haus Böcking, where Goethe once stayed. Traben is also home to highly imaginative turn-of-the-century Art Nouveau buildings designed by the architect Bruno Möhring, such as the Villa Breucker and the Hotel Bellevue. Further upstream, the main valley leads into another double town: Bernkastel-Kues, the seat of the Moselland eG company, the largest association of viticulturalists on the Moselle open to the public (wine tasting included – but you should take the opportunity of visiting smaller establishments as well to buy a liquid souvenir). Niklas von Kues was born here in Kues, a German universal genius of the late Middle Ages, a scientist and philosopher of religion, vicar general in Rome. He died in the year 1464 and bequeathed the St. Nikolaus-Hospital Foundation to his hometown. Today, one of the foundation buildings houses the Moselle Museum of Wine, along with the famous scholar's library. Revenue from his vineyards still contributes towards the running of a local old people's residence. Further up the hill, there is a wonderful view from the ruins of the mediaeval Castle Landshut down onto the town and its splendid vineyards.

Germany's oldest city Trier, is the cultural high point of a trip down the Moselle. Founded in the year 16 BCE by the Romans as Augusta Treverorum, it enjoyed particular significance in the fourth century as capital of the West Roman Empire, and was so richly endowed with representational buildings that you'll need at least one day to do them justice. One Roman resident of the city named Ausonius wrote an enthusiastic hymn of praise dedicated to the Moselle in 371 BCE. Based on its wealth of classical Roman and mediaeval art (Porta Nigra, Palastaula of Emperor Constantine, imperial thermal baths, amphitheatre, artworks in the Regional State Museum, Cathedral and Church of Our Lady), Trier has received UNESCO World Heritage Site status. Even the old bridge spanning the Moselle rests on Roman foundations. Trier is also a centre of wine and sparkling wine production. About one quarter of German sparkling wines are produced here.

The castle of castles: Eltz

There are several options when it comes to travelling back downstream: by car on the Hunsrück-Höhenstrasse route (only about half the distance needed by the riverside roads in the valley), by boat with more time to appreciate the scenery, or even on foot along the Moselle Upland Footpath (see info box on p. 97 for further information on these suggestions). Regardless of the route chosen, travellers in the lower reaches of the Moselle Valley should take a break close to the town of Karden, near Moselkern, for a little excursion into the Middle Ages: 35 minutes upstream through the Elz Valley, through woods and past slate rock-faces to Castle Eltz. Situated on a 70-metre-high outcrop, the four-storeyed castle is

an impressive sight, a densely structured mesh of turrets and towers.
Castle Eltz is a so-called "Ganerbenburg", a castle belonging to a community of joint heirs. The core of the castle dates back to the 12th century, when it was a fortified structure but not a fortress – the castle lords were careful to maintain diplomatic relations in preference to conflict. It was strategically built on a road linking the Moselle – one of the most important trade routes in the German Empire – to the Eifel region and the fertile collective municipality of Maifeld.
The castle expanded gradually, in particular during the 15th century when new half-timbered structures and towers were added. Today, it is open to the public daily from April to November 1: the Eltz family spends most of the year in Eltville. The tour guides are good at contextualising local and family history – and valuable works of art are also on show: a "Madonna with Child and Grapes", by Lucas Cranach, delicate 15th-century frescoes in one of the bedrooms, a fully equipped castle kitchen, household tools from various eras, wall hangings, ceramics and last but not least, the treasure chamber (extra admission fee) with masterpieces of gold- and silversmith work, including a Diana with horse and dog in the form of a 'double beaker'. You'll be able to enjoy a good local wine in the castle – served in less auspicious vessel of course.

TRADITION AND PLEASURE

Located directly on the Moselle, the Hotel Noss has been run by the same family for 100 years. 31 rooms and three restaurants are available in addition to the Bistro Café Royal. All food is prepared with high-quality products and served with exquisite wines.

Hotel Noss
Moselpromenade 17, 56812 Cochem
tel.: +49 (0)2671/3612, fax: 5366
www.hotel-noss.de

FOR MORE INFORMATION ON THE MOSELLE VALLEY AND CASTLE ELTZ

Tourist-Information Ferienland Cochem
tel.: +49 (0)2671/60040
Mosellandtouristik GmbH
tel.: +49 (0)6531/97330 and 2091, fax: 2093
Websites: www.cochem.de,
www.mosellandtouristik.de
www.burg-eltz.de

26 The Rheingau Region around Winkel and Castle Johannisberg

The discovery of the late harvest

It is 1755, when ladies wore hooped skirts and men sported pigtails. The viticulturalists around the former monastery of Johannisberg were subject to the rule of the Prince Bishop of Fulda Monastery, obliged to wait for the Prince Bishop's express permission before they begin harvesting the grapes. Desperation and catastrophe: the messenger from Fulda was delayed, the overripe grapes withered and began to rot on the vine! Finally, permission arrived, and the grapes were harvested. Their "noble rot" produced a wine which delights experts: the very first 'Spätlese' (late harvest).

Centre: In the heart of the Rheingau: the wine-trading town of Eltville.
Below: vines above, cellars below: the Rheingau has its own special subterranean culture. Opposite: its tower may look defiant, but the wonderfully located Johannisberg Castle boasts elegance as well.

The Rheingau region is densely packed with vineyards stretching down the slopes towards the Rhine, vines reaching up to the sun. At this point in its course, the Rhine describes a 30-kilometre meander from east to west, so that nearly all the vineyards are south facing, tucked up close in a relatively small area, interspersed with villages all connected to each other by roads and footpaths.

275 years ago, Church authorities decreed that only the Riesling vine be cultivated in the area. Even today, about 80% of the local wines are Rieslings, a vine of the highest quality. Its aroma, with its characteristically fine acidity, is redolent – depending on situation and vintage – of peaches, apricots, or honey. If you're prepared to wait some years before uncorking a Riesling, you'll find that its quality has improved. No wonder that experts and aficionados from all over the world appreciate this wine. Sometimes even Riesling wines growing abroad are called "Riesling Johannisberg".

The River Rhine flows directly past the village houses built down on its shores – a sight of great majesty and the focus of the local landscape. In mild winters, the river wraps itself in mist, picturesquely accentuating trees and shrubs and concealing the island of Mariannenaue, a nature reserve to the east of Winkel. In the spring however, the river swells, bursts its banks, floods roads and jetties, lapping the gardens and forecourts of

Above: half-timbered cosiness in Oestrich. Centre: The Drosselgasse in Rüdesheim, an El Dorado of wine tasting for millions of tourists from all over the world. Below: for the more discerning palate: the cellars of the Eiserhof in Oestrich. Opposite: Brömserburg Castle in Rüdesheim is home to "Siegfried's Mechanical Music Cabinett".

local residents. Nonetheless, the wine benefits from the river all year round: in the summer, the glittering waters refract sunlight, and in the winter, the residual warmth in the water warms the cooler land. According to legend, it was Charlemagne who noticed that the snow on the riverbank opposite the Imperial Stronghold of Ingelheim in the Rheingau region was melting far more quickly than that under his feet and insisted that the Benedictine monks on the Johannisberg devote their energies to the cultivation of wine.

The monastery looks back over a turbulent history. It was plundered during the Reformation, when it was caught in the crossfire of the Peasants' War – when the poor peasants apparently welcomed the chance to drink good wine – and was dissolved before the outbreak of the Thirty Years War. It changed hands several times before it became the property of the Prince Bishop of Fulda. Winemaking was always an integral part of the estate business, and the quality improved steadily, even when the property was gifted to the famous German Chancellor Prince von Metternich in return for services rendered during the Congress of Vienna. The Metternich family is still in charge of castle affairs and wine making. Guided tours are available through the medieval cellars, where visitors can check out rows of wooden wine barrels, admire a collection of rare wines and sample the contents of the traditionally slender Rheingau bottles (known as "Flutes"). There is a wonderful view over the entire area from the tavern's summer terrace. More energetic visitors will appreciate the network of public footpaths between Wiesbaden and Lorch linking thirteen valley and seven hillside parishes whose villages and towns are synonymous with vineyards and locations that the true expert will be able to identify simply by taste – or so it is said. A special kind of dense brushwood, grows along the valley ridges. It was originally planted in the Middle Ages to keep off robbers. Today, it keeps cold air away from the upper slopes.

Romantic wine-growing villages

Eltville is famous for its rose-lined romantic alleys, its castle, its courtyards and its Gutenberg Museum (the impoverished inventor of mechanical printing found a home here in his old age). A little further up in the hills, the little town of Kiedrich delights sightseers with its picturesque medieval flair and the prospect of a visit to the nearby Cistercian Monastery of Eberbach, centre of the Hesse State Wineries and famous for its atmospheric cellar vaults. Geisenheim is known for its Grape Breeding Institute, Rüdesheim is more famous still for its popular, kiss-me-quick Drosselgasse, which offers guests the chance to overnight in wine barrels and a cable care ride to the Niederwald Monument (1877–83) whose statuesque figure of Germania might be considered pop art today.

Assmannshausen has been attracting famous visitors since the 19th century (a who's who of these is listed in the Guest House "Krone"): its speciality, however, is not a Riesling but an excellent red wine made from late-ripening Burgundy grapes.

An Olympian guest

"Through stately lands these waters run/whose skies are bright, whose courses wide/And well before the journey's done/they take brief rest by Winkel's side."

Goethe loved the little town of Winkel, located about half way along that part of the Rhine Valley known as the Rheingau. He came here in the autumn of 1814 to stay with his friend, the writer Brentano, on whose estates visitors can still visit the little rooms in which Goethe spent his time, disturbing his hosts' daily routine with the entrenched habits of an old man. The owners still celebrate their famous guest with a wine named after the poet: "Goethewein" (Goethe Wine). The salon culture cultivated by the Romantic movement in the form of musical and poetry evenings – Bettina Brentano was a guest and mentions night-time excursions on the water – has been revived today by Angela von Brentano, whose sophisticated cultural events have proved very popular.

Goethe's presence can still be felt everywhere in Winkel: in the old wine restaurant located in an old stone house, on the walking trails leading up the hill to Vollrads Castle, home and vineyard estate of the Matuschka-Greiffenclau family, with its mediaeval tower. Another path leading through the vineyards in the direction of Geisenheim passes by Johannisberg Castle, where our little tour of the Rheingau ends. Much has been left out, such as the elegant city of Wiesbaden, or the town of Hochheim, situated further eastwards, which was once so popular with English wine-lovers that they referred to every white wine as a "hoc." The Rheingau welcomes its guests with countless hotels, inns and restaurants.

4 STARS ON THE RHINE

The generously proportioned Hotel Schwann has been welcoming visitors since 1628. Situated by the Rhine (with river-side terrace), the four-star hotel has 54 rooms and pampers its guests with candle-light wine tastings in its vaulted cellars. Good, creative cuisine.

Hotel Schwan
Rheinallee 5, 65375 Oestrich-Winkel
tel.: +49 (0)6723/8090, fax: 7820
www.hotel-schwan.de

FOR MORE INFORMATION ON THE RHEINGAU

Verkehrsamt Oestrich-Winkel
tel.: +49 (0) 6723/19433
Rheingau-Taunus Information
tel.: +49 (0)6723/99550, Fax 995555
Köln-Düsseldorfer Rheinschiffahrt AG (river cruise company)
tel.: +49 (0)221/2088318, fax: 2088345
websites: www.rheingau-taunus-info.de, www.k.d.com, www.WeinlandRheingau.de, www.rheingau-musik-festival.de

27 An Artistic Awakening in Darmstadt

Art Nouveau flourishes on the Mathildenhöhe

Seekers of innovation and change sometimes leave impressive footprints. Those on the Mathildenhöhe (Mathilda's Heights) in Darmstadt are impressive indeed: flamboyant buildings that attract visitors from all over the world. Have you ever seen a tower quite like this wide, violet and dark-red brick structure, tapering off, as it rises upwards, into a coppered verdigris, five-fingered gable? It is the "Wedding Tower", a symbolic gift following the marriage of the last Grand Duke, Ernst Ludwig von Hesse and Rhine with Eleonore von Solm-Hohensolm-Lich.

Centre: Art Nouveau portal of irreproachable pedigree: form, colour and wrought-iron lines. Below: artistic intimacies at the Wedding Tower.
Opposite: The Wedding Tower, a powerful architectural gesture. Counterpoint on the Mathildenhöhe: the Russian-Orthodox Church.

The very names are reminiscent of old, faded photos. Did those involved anticipate the end of an era? Yet by 1905, when the wedding took place, modernity had already made its mark on the Mathildenhöhe – sanctioned, indeed, commissioned by the Grand Duke himself. A new way of life was to combine beauty and functionality – the prerequisite for a happy life. Over the course of about a dozen years a residential district was developed around the Ernst-Ludwig-House (1900/1901) and the Wedding Tower (1908), a conglomerate of houses, studios, gardens and sculptures.
In the aftermath of two cataclysmic world wars, not many were able to muster much enthusiasm for the whimsy of Art Nouveau, but these examples of Art Nouveau architecture have remained to inspire and delight visitors. The Ernst Ludwig House, formerly used as a studio, has been carefully restored. Flanked by two majestic Ludwig Habich sculptures, the barrel-vaulted, intricately ornamented entrance extends a quasi-sacred welcome. Exhibits on show in the interior include objects of daily use fashioned in the Art Nouveau style: furniture, glasswork, paintings, friezes. The Darmstadt Artists' Colony promoted the production not only of expensive artworks but also aimed to improve industrial design and manufacture.
It had been the Grand Duke's intention to create an artists' colony in Darmstadt when he summoned the architect Josep

Maria Olbrich (1867–1908) to the city in 1899. Olbrich arrived here flushed with the successes of the Vienna Secession and his inimitable style is evident on the portal of the Ernst-Ludwig-House. Six artists joined him in Darmstadt, some of whom achieved a similar measure of fame: Peter Behrens, for example, who later worked in Berlin. The others were Rudolf Bosselt, Paul Bürck, Hans Christiansen, Ludwig Habich and Patriz Huber. Within two years, their combined efforts had led to the first exhibition on the Mathildenhöhe, dedicated to presenting the new style. The recently built houses were exhibited to the public before being inhabited – and not only by the wealthy. Some models were built for people of more limited means. Unfortunately, some of these model dwellings have not survived and those that have cannot be viewed from the inside since they are in use by various cultural institutions. Nonetheless, it's well worth taking a closer look at the Mathildenhöhe, starting perhaps with the Wedding Tower, where the room of the Grand Duke and Duchess may be viewed (unless temporarily in use by the registrar for weddings).

To the south of the tower two paths, the Alexandraweg and the Christiansweg, run parallel from east to west to the Glückert House with its curved gambrel roof and omega arches, followed by the Deiters House and the Habich House, the first flat roof house built by Olbrich for the colony based on south European models.

An interesting counterpoint to the prevailing Art Nouveau may be found on the western edge of the Mathildenhöhe, where the Russian Chapel was built in a historicising style by Tsar Nicholas II in honour of his wife, a Princess of Hesse, and consecrated in 1899. The couple was later shot by Bolshevists along with their children: the building remains as a sad memorial.

The neighbouring grove of plane trees, decades older than the colony itself, is a good spot to take a rest. The reliefs and sculptures are the work of Bernhard Hoetger, an artist closely associated with Bremen and Worpswede.

INDIVIDUAL AND FAMILIAR

The small, individually managed city Hotel Mathildenhöhe is located close to the artists' colony and Art Nouveau buildings, but also conveniently situated for the city centre. The management fulfils all wishes and welcomes families with children. The breakfast buffet provides a good start to the day.

Hotel Mathildenhöhe
Spessartring 53, 64287 Darmstadt
tel.: +49 (0)6151/49840, fax: 498450
www.hotel-mathildenhoehe.de

FOR FURTHER INFORMATION ON DARMSTADT

City tours etc.
ProRegio Darmstadt
tel. +49 (0)6151/6428
Ticketshop/Information – Louisencenter
tel.: +49 (0)6151/2799999, fax: 2799998
Websites: www.darmstadt.de, www.proregio-darmstadt.de, www.hlmd.de (Hessisches Landesmuseum), www.mathildenhoehe.info.html, www.kunstmarkt.de

Centre: On the River Neckar, opposite the old town, close to the Philosophenweg. Below: The Mariensäule on the Corn Market exudes Baroque flair. Opposite: View over the River Neckar and the Karl Theodor Bridge up to the castle, the first such construction built in the German Renaissance.

28 The Myth: Heidelberg

River and mountain, castle and bridge

It's not difficult to get a bird's eye perspective onto this town, down onto the gardens and the wooded valley by the river: the mountain offers a perfect outlook. To get to the top of the Königstuhl just hop onto the funicular, change halfway up into the quietly groaning cabins of the historic cable car (in perfect working order and recently restored to its early 20th-century wooden splendour) and you'll soon find yourself looking out over a splendid vista.

From up here, the view encompasses the tightly packed roofs and church spires of the old town abutting the River Neckar. The green fields of the Neuenheimer Feld beyond the river are used by students for recreational purposes, and adjacent to these the modern buildings of an old university (founded in 1386) gleam in the sunlight. Further down river, a wide swathe of uncluttered industrial landscape spreads to the horizon.

Heidelberg – much extolled, romantically acclaimed, some might say mythologized, by a host of literary greats from Germany and beyond: Goethe, Brentano, Hauff, Eichendorff, Mark Twain, to name but a few. Today, the international babble of tongues to be heard in the city's pedestrian zone is proof that the town has remained popular with more than just poetry fans. With over 600,000 overnight stays, the local tourist authority "Kongress und Tourismus GmbH" has every reason to insist upon Heidelberg's continued allure, above all for Americans and East Asians. Not all visitors come in search of old-Heidelberg nostalgia. The far-flung members of the Heidelberg Club International (HCI) are more interested in the city's reputation as a centre for science and innovation, with particular emphasis on bio- and information technologies.

Catchphrases and answers

Why then, is this town so famous? Try these epithets for size: landscape, youth, student life, sensual and spiritual experience, the mild climate, the red stone castle ruins, the charming beauty of the old town, a feeling for tradition coupled with an optimistic embrace of the future …

They stop, the wanderers, enchanted. Who'd walk on now and leave this sphere?

Above: Overgrown ruins on the Schlossberg. Centre: A throwback to the times of Emperor William: the corporations or student associations. Below: Market place with town hall and fountain. Right: The Hauptstrasse, Heidelberg's principal shopping mile. Opposite: The castle and the towers of the old bridge.

The vision, in their dreams implanted,
Called out to each that home was near,
Not once was any man deceived.
T'was Heidelberg that they'd perceived." (Eichendorff)

Let's go to the castle, whose empty windows and shattered tower are a monument to the horrors of war in the late 17th century. Yet it shines still in the evening light, occasionally reflecting the sparkle of a firework display and continues to provide a popular venue for performances of German classics such as "Urfaust". Visitors still come in droves to look at the great barrel located on its premises and shudder when they imagine the strange concoction brewed in its cavernous depths for the delectation of dukes. The castle is surrounded by gardens and a park in which the aged Goethe came to muse on the bittersweet delight of his love for a younger woman and where the object of his delight, Marianne von Willemer, composed verses of her own, now inscribed on a stone tablet situated in the western part of the gardens. The view from the castle grounds onto the old town is much better than that from the Königsstuhl: it appears far closer, and more enticing. How charming, to live under those pointed roofs. The river Neckar gleams below and the sun's rays glitter on an almost transparent solar cruise boat – a technical innovation, the largest of its kind worldwide. Where else do past and future merge so seamlessly? In the year 1815, as Goethe and his muse were composing their poems, the destruction of the castle and the city of Heidelberg in the late 17th century was still fairly recent: Louis XIV of France insisted that the Palatinate region was part of his heritage, based on the fact that his sister-in-law Liselotte was herself a sister of the deceased Prince Elector. She had spent a happy, carefree childhood in Heidelberg Castle, and left behind many letters in Versailles testifying to her exceptional temperament,

good humour, kindness – and to an eloquence characterized by the local turn-of-phrase. Confined to the golden cage of Versailles, she was powerless in the face of her brother in-law's brutality. It is strange that the destruction of the castle detracted so little from its charms. In 1779, Duke Karl August von Sachsen-Weimar, Goethe's friend wrote: "I crept around in the beautiful old ruins. It was wonderful."

Today, the ruins are open to the public and once visitors have admired the pharmacy, the barrel, the statues of former rulers and architectural details, many like to relax with a short walk under the grand old trees in the castle gardens. Unhappily, the Renaissance garden laid down by Hortus Palatinus with flowers and a fountain can only be seen today on old illustrations.

Like the castle, the Karl-Theodor Bridge was built with red sandstone. Unlike the castle, it still stands intact, named after the Wittelsbach Duke, heir to the Electoral Palatinate, who also inherited Munich and Bavaria at the end of the 18th century and departed thence, taking with him his extensive collection of fine art. The Duke stands proudly on the bridge, optically counterpoised on the other side by Pallas Athena, the Greek goddess of learning.

The Baroque buildings housing the university are the main architectural element of the old town. Some of the faculties have emigrated to newer buildings on the Neuenheimer Feld on the other side of the river but it would be a pity if they were all to go. Student social life still takes place largely in the old town: the cosy old pubs are popular not only with the conservative brand of young person that sometimes tends towards right-wing extremism but also with the more modern, third-millennia students. The university remains the heart and soul of a cosmopolitan, open-minded city whose students retain a lifelong affection for their alma mater.

A VIEW ONTO THE CASTLE

A new hotel in an old house situated close to the arches of an even older bridge. Yet the guests remain undisturbed by the hordes of tourists, thanks to a secluded courtyard. Fans of handpicked modern design will appreciate the interior, complemented by large-scale black and white panorama photos of Heidelberg. Several rooms offer views of the castle. Good, unpretentious food is served in the adjoining Restaurant Nepomuk.

Hotel Zur Alten Brücke
Obere Neckarstrasse 2, 69117 Heidelberg
tel.: +49 (0)6221/739130, www.Hotel-zur-Alten-Bruecke.de, parking available.

FOR FURTHER INFORMATION ON HEIDELBERG

Tourist Information in the main station
tel.: +49 (0)6221/19433, fax: 1388111
Websites: www.tourismus-heidelberg.de, www.heidelberg-aktuell.de, www.heidelberg-kongresse.de

29 Bamberg – Franconia's Most Beautiful World Heritage Site

Riders and large ladies

He keeps watch over the faithful from on high, looking down onto bowed heads in the cathedral shadows. Almost as famous as Michelangelo's David in Florence, the Bamberg Horseman is considered the epitome of courtly breeding in whose expression and posture an anonymous sculptor immortalized the fascinating aura of lightness coupled with extreme concentration. Scholars can only guess at the horseman's identity – was it a real-life person or an idealized vision? Recent art historical research has come to the conclusion that the sculptor modelled his subject on King Stephen of Hungary, brother-in-law of the city's founder Emperor Henry II.

Saint Kunigunde, King Henry II's wife and city patron, looks out onto the old town from the Maxplatz. The colourful vegetable market is a popular local meeting point. Opposite: the splendid façade of the Old Town Hall on an artificially created island in the River Regnitz.

The large recumbent female by the Colombian artist Fernando Botero on permanent loan to the city of Bamberg is about seven or eight hundred years younger than the horseman. Botero is known for his generously proportioned and yet graceful ladies, and for his ability to make them look energetic rather than sluggish.

Some years ago Bamberg's art and antique dealers hit on the idea of putting Botero's lady on a raft and sending her down the River Regnitz as a kind of happening. Unfortunately, the well-endowed bronze lady soon sank. Happily, she survived her impromptu bath and soon returned to her pedestal on the Heumark.

One or two visits to Bamberg should be enough to convince visitors that these two very different sculptures reflect very different but equally appealing local traits characteristic of this uniquely beautiful city and its inhabitants. The town has everything to offer and does so with open hands: a cathedral and beer cellars, Episcopal rose gardens and literary fantasies from the era of Romanticism, miracle-working legend and hard scientific enterprise. Bamberg has seen its fair share of fighting and war, of fires and crimes – not least, the brutal murder of King Philip of Swabia by his rival Otto von Wittelsbach, which took place in 1208 in Bamberg's Episcopal palace. But the locals have always succeeded in

Old Bamberg: Hochzeitshaus (Wedding House) and Alter Kranen on the Regnitz (above), momento mori on a grave in St. Michael's (centre), half-timbered structures in the old Episcopal Palace on the cathedral hill date back to the Middle Ages (below). Opposite: "Little Venice" and the Old Town Hall.

maintaining their city's beauty and welcoming lifestyle.

Bamberg has become particularly popular with visitors since World War II when it was one of the few German towns to escape large-scale fire damage. There was death and destruction here as elsewhere, but only 20% of buildings were lost. The fact that such a city (and one favoured by emperors) retains a sense of continuity, makes visiting Bamberg a particularly attractive proposition. In 1994, the city was declared a World Heritage Site by UNESCO.

One thousand years of history

Just a short walk up the hill from the green river valley takes visitors right into the centre of Bamberg's past, where emperors, bishops and churches wrote history. The cathedral, the Renaissance façade of the Episcopal residence and those of the new, Baroque Episcopal residence, the rose gardens beyond with a view onto the city and the river – all this combines to create a unique insight into over 1000 years of Bamberg history. Archaeological excavations have determined that prior to the year 1000, this spot was home to the seat of the Babenberger family, from whom the name Bamberg derives. Castle Babenberg was a wedding gift bestowed by the Bavarian Duke Henry IV upon Kunigunde, the daughter of a Luxembourg Duke. In 1002, the Duke was elected King Henry II of Germany and shortly afterwards, he began preparing the foundation of a new diocese in Bamberg, which led to the city's increase in influence and importance. This era was the apogee of the Imperial Church, which had been strengthened and supported by kings and emperors since the time of Otto the Great, who intended it as a counterweight to the ever ambitious nobility. In 1014, Henry II had himself crowned emperor by Pope Benedict the eighth. He was the last emperor from the Ottonian Dynasty.

The Bambergers have Henry and his Kunigunde to thank for the rise in their city's fortunes. Both the king and his wife were canonised and their thankful subjects spared no expense in having them portrayed time and again in churches and palaces. Tilman Riemenschneider, one of the most significant artists of the late Gothic era, created the most beautiful of these when he immortalized them in two life-size figures, carved for the couple's splendid sarcophagus.

Little Pegnitz Island in the River Regnitz – a jewel in itself, with its leafy trails – affords one of the best views of the city for those willing to climb the tower of the miniature castle of Geyerswörth. From this vantage point, one can look across to the Old Town Hall, audaciously situated on an even smaller island when it was built in the 14th century, and further beyond to the nooks and alleys of the enchanting old town, and then upwards onto the spires crowning the seven hills on which the city was built.

A lust for life: theatres and beer cellars

Bamberg is also known for its lively, and recently carefully enlarged E.T.A. Hoffmann Theatre. Hoffmann was a poet and master story-teller of fantastic tales who came to the city in 1808 to take up a position as director of music at this very theatre. He took lodgings in a narrow little house opposite the theatre, fell unhappily in love and left Bamberg in 1813. But his presence remains and thousands now come to climb the narrow stairs of the Hoffmann Museum, to view his tiny chambers and read excerpts from his work.

Friends of classical and modern music alike are drawn to the "Sinfonie an der Regnitz" concert hall, situated outside the old town (with plenty of parking spaces). The old town itself is reserved largely for pedestrians, especially the area around the Grüner Markt and the Hauptwachstrasse, the cathedral and the New Episcopal Palace, allowing visitors to stand back and look upwards onto the façades of churches and splendid townhouses without risking life and limb.

Beware, however, of cars in the Judenstrasse, home to the splendid Böttingerhaus, and also around the moated castle Concordia down by the river.

Bamberg is a city of exquisite churches and well-endowed museums, of antiques and fashion, arts and crafts, not to mention locally produced delicacies and Franconian wines. An astonishing number of private breweries still produce local beers, including a Bamberg specialty: Rauchbier (smoked beer). Where there are breweries, there are also beer cellars: one of Bamberg's most beautiful is the Greifenklau Cellar on the Kaulberg Hill.

Bamberg also has a university with the attendant university life: gesticulating students and/or music. "Jazzclub", for example, entertains its guest with live music at the weekend. What would the emperor think?

A WINE HOUSE WITH TRADITION

The Romantic-Hotel Messerschmitt, founded in 1832, has an excellent cuisine and 32 comfortable rooms. It is conveniently situated on the edge of the old town, with parking spaces.

Hotel Messerschmitt
Lange Strasse 41, 96047 Bamberg
tel.: +49 (0)951/27866, fax: 26141
www.hotel-messerschmitt.de

FOR MORE INFORMATION ON BAMBERG

Bamberg Tourismus & Kongress Service
tel.: +49 (0)951/871161, reservation hotline +49 (0)951/871154 (also holiday appartments), fax: 871960
Websites: www.tourismus.bamberg.de

30 On the new "Franconian Trail"

Franconian forests: for ramblers and for dreamers

As the poet said: "These woods are lovely, dark and deep..." By woods, we don't mean just any woods, but specifically, the woods of Franconia, and even more particularly, the Franconian Forests. Where exactly are they? As any Franconian will tell you, they occupy the exact centre of Germany. Not of interest for those living on the coast or the Rhine, but a point of honour for Franconians.

Centre: cosy market-square in Kronach's old town. Below: coat of arms on the Town Hall. Opposite above: hiking through fields near Wellesberg/Wallenfels. Below: view onto the Höllental near Naila from the "King David" viewing platform, 160 metres above the valley with hydro electric power plant; and the "Devil's Bridge" in the nature reserve.

In the north, the Franconian forests border on Thuringia, part of the border zone during the GDR era. The green of the forest is the dominant colour on these wooded slopes: none of Franconia's large cities are located within the forest boundaries. Würzburg is situated to the west, Bamberg to the southwest, Bayreuth to the south and Nuremberg even further south. However, the Franconian forests are proud to encompass the towns of Kronach, famous for its huge Rosenberg fortress and the "Faust" festival, as well as Kulmbach, the capital of Franconian brewing. It is also home to the first large segment of a hiking trail known as the "Frankenweg" (Franconian Trail).

Rambling from the Rennsteig to the Swabian Alps

Despite its generic name, the Franconian Trail is the youngest of the local long-distance trails. Opened in the autumn of 2004, it goes from the Rennsteig to the Swabian Alps, covering a challenging 520 kilometres through the valleys of Franconia's Central German Uplands into the upper Main Valley, through the caves and crevices of Franconian Switzerland to the castles of the Frankish Alb, turning west to skirt the Franconian lakes and winding its way through the Altmühl Valley, before turning sharply south again once it has passed through the "Roman city" of Weissenburg and finally arriving at the quaint town of Harburg overlooking the River Wörnitz.

What more could any rambler wish for than such a massed presentation of Franconia's splendid landscapes? Why did it take so long to get this trail established? Our guess is simply that it required unusual amounts of energy and dynamism to put together one long trail from all the little paths criss-crossing the region, not to mention the approval of all the local tourist associations: the Frankenwaldverein, the Fränkische-Schweiz-Verein, and the Fränkische Albverein have pooled their

Above: Renaissance portal on Kronach's Rosenberg fortress. Centre: The old town, rich in half-timbered structures. Below: Fountain on the Marienplatz in Kronach. Right above: The moated castle of Mitwitz, near Kronach. Opposite above: crossing the castle moat into the Rosenberg fortress. Opposite below: the Ködeltalsperre reservoir lake.

resources to ensure optimal sign-posting. The Franconian Trail was the first Bavarian trail to receive the green seal of approval from the German Rambling Association.

There is also plenty of precisely formulated information material available: German thoroughness is well in evidence, for example, in the brochures published by the Franconian Forest Nature Reserve, which not only suggests specific daily itineraries, but also recommends accommodation and how to get there, with distances specified from the Franconian Trail. Data is also provided on changes in altitude (which affect 123 kilometres of trail). The Frankenwaldverein has published a rambling guide: "Der Frankenweg im Frankenwald" (Franconian Trail in the Franconian Forest), with maps and photos.

Hirschsprung, Höllental and Handweber

If you want to start at the beginning, make your way to the village of Untereichenstein on the River Selbitz, close to Thuringia, where the Rennsteig Ridge Walk turns into the Franconian Trail. It's not long before the path starts going steeply uphill, providing panoramic views such as that from the "King David Heights" onto deep and densely wooded valleys, home to a gallery dug by miners and named after the biblical figure of King David.

From here it's not far to the first views onto the Höllental valley: the best of these is afforded by the Hirschsprung, a rocky outcrop crowned with a life-size sculpture of a leaping deer. According to legend, the deer jumped into the Selbitz Valley to save itself from a hunting party led by Margrave Friedrich zu

Bayreuth (1735–63). Rather than follow suit, we continue down the steep path until we get to the old mining village of Blechschmidtenhammer, where we take a break in a local hostel.

In the Höllental valley, place names evoking the devil and hell refer to a local legend chronicling the meeting between a courageous charcoal burner and the devil, whist the remains of technical facility hark testify to the arduous beginnings of industrialization in the 19th century.

From here, the trail continues on through fields and woods, occasionally passing through villages as we make our way through the wide terrain known as Handweber Frankenwald (Weavers' Franconian Forest), once dominated by the domestic weaving industry, documented in the simple Handicrafts Museum located in the little village of Marlesreuth, where the local weaver Adolf Franz, cap on head, skilfully demonstrates the art of weaving.

In this, or in like manner, the first of six walking days on the Franconian Trail comes to an end after roughly 25 km of solid rambling. There has been much to see between start and finish under open skies, and by rushing streams far from the occasionally distant sounds of traffic encountered when crossing the occasional road. Whether talking or walking in companionable silence, we have felt the wind in our hair and smelled the earthy forest floors warming under the midday sun.

Enchanting Altfranken (Old Franconia): Kronach

The forests are beautiful enough, but many Franconian towns and villages are also well worth a visit. Take our tip and try and see Kronach from above, with a view down onto its old Franconian structures: the Flossherrenhaus and Annakapelle, the Hexenturm (witches' tower), its fountains and alleys, old cobblestones and five-hundred-year-old soup kitchen for the sick and the poor. The medieval fortress Rosenberg – Kronach's Gothic Pentagon – is nearly as big as the entire old town, with space enough to house the Franconian Art Gallery with work by famous German artists of the Middle Ages such as Lucas Cranach the Elder (who was born here), Tilman Riemenschneider and Hans von Kulmach. It also stages the "Faust" Open Air Theatre Festival, with Goethe's Mephisto character played by a woman. The next castle is just a one-day hike to Kulmbach on the Main, where you can visit the splendid castle of Plassenburg, with armies of tin soldiers and other old rarities. With attractions such as these, it won't be long before the Franconian Trail takes its place alongside Thuringia's Rennsteig Ridge Walk as a "cult" ramble.

FRANCONIAN SNUGNESS

With its attention to the comfort of body and soul, the double-hotel ensemble Pfarrhof & Am Pförtchen in Kronach's old town welcomes its guests with all manner of services: laundry, luggage, bike rental. Nothing is too much trouble.

Pfarrhof & Am Pförtchen
Amtsgerichtsstrasse 12, 96317 Kronach
tel.: +49 (0)9261/504590, fax: 5045999
www.stadthotel-pfarrhof.de

FOR MORE INFORMATION ON THE FRANCONIAN TRAIL AND FRANCONIAN FORESTS

Frankenwald Tourismus. Service Center
tel.: +49 (0)9261/60150, fax: 601515
websites: www.frankenweg.de, www.frankenwald.tourismus.de, www.naturpark-frankenwald.de, www.kronach.de, www.kulmbach.de, www.faust-festspiele.de

Above and opposite above: Rothenburg is world famous, especially for its half-timber and gablehouses, located on Market Square. Opposite below: the historical Roedergate.

31 Rothenburg ob der Tauber

Comfort amid churches and cobblestones

Although the little town situated high above the river Tauber has not been accorded World Heritage Site status by UNESCO, it is certainly world-famous, so famous indeed that other towns borrow its name to advertise their own charms: Landsberg am Lech for example, refers to itself as the "Bavarian Rothenburg", whilst the little town of Beilstein on the Moselle calls itself a miniature Rothenburg and the town of Hornburg in Lower Saxony justifies its use of the epithet "Rothenburg of the North" by insisting on the wealth of its half-timbered structures.

The competition, however, lags far behind the original. Only Rothenburg can claim such an enchanting location, with its walls, its gates and its towers rising over the Tauber Valley. Few other towns can boast such a wealth of historically significant buildings, both secular and sacred, within its walls – especially when viewed as an urban ensemble. Rothenburg knows the value of maintaining both the appearance and atmosphere of historical authenticity and has relegated 20th- and 21st- century developments to districts outside the historic town walls.

These walls have been so well preserved that visitors will feel enclosed and protected when walking through the small alleys and passing by secluded corners. The cobblestones under one's feet, the sound of splashing water from the fountains: strolling through Rothenburg is a walk through the ages, from mediaeval churches such as the 13th-century Franciscan church and the 14th-century high Gothic church of St James (with its Altar of the Holy Blood by Tilman Riemenschneider), past old town houses and craftsmen's dwellings, arriving finally at the half-timbered gables of the Jagstheimer House and the Meat and Dance House on Market Square.

The lively crowds milling around Rothenburg's Renaissance Town Hall come from all over the world: Japanese, Korean, and more recently Chinese have joined the British and American visitors eager to see where Rothenburg's mayor presented the Catholic General Tilly with a three-quarter litre tankard of wine. It was 1631, the Thirty Years' War was raging, Rothenburg had been conquered and the general was threatening to lay waste to the town – unless someone managed to drink down the wine in one go. The mayor stepped up and

succeeded thereby, saving Rothenburg. Every year, the "Master Drink" spectacle is performed in memory of this feat. Further evidence of war and peace has been preserved in the ancient vaults of Rothenburg's Town Hall. Visitors can also climb the tower for a splendid view over the roofs, the city walls, the towers and spires and further out over the countryside beyond.

The walkway along the battlements of the city walls is open to the public from the Klingenbastei to the Kobolzer Tor, a distance of about two-and-a-half kilometres. Countless treasures await you attention in the churches and museums.

HOTEL RECOMMENDATION

Badischer Hof,
Am Sonnenplatz,
97941 Tauberbischosheim,
tel.: +49 (0)9341/9880, fax 988200,
www.hotelbadischerhof.de

FOR MORE INFORMATION:

Tourist information Rothenburg ob der Tauber
Marktplatz 2
91541 Rothenburg o.T.
tel.: +49 (0)9861-404800
www.rothenburg.de

Church spires tower over an almost medieval vista: quiet alleys lead off from the marketplace and town hall uphill towards the castle.

32 Quedlinburg Delivered

Half-timbered houses and early german kings

This old city on the northern edge of the Harz mountains, home to kings and emperors, is the mecca of half-timbered structures, over 1000 of which survived from the time of their construction between the 15th to 18th centuries until 1990, when the decision was taken to restore as many of them as possible. The results are astonishing: one house after another was painstakingly restored. UNESCO's 1994 decision to bestow World Heritage Status on the city continues to discourage modern, synthetic shop-front façades from destroying the seamlessly historic old town ensemble.

Quedlinburg is a city of kings and emperors. Henry I, the first king of Germany's medieval Ottonian dynasty, convened imperial diets in Quedlinburg. Situated next to the renaissance castle, the Collegiate Church St. Servatius was consecrated in the year 1129. Its columned portal and crypt belong to the earliest masterpieces of German Romanesque architecture.

HOTEL RECOMMENDATION: Romantik Hotel Theophano, Markt 14, 06484 Quedlinburg, tel.: +49 (0)3946/96300, fax: 963036,
E-Mail: theophano@t-online.de

Punting in the Spree Forest: a favourite summer pastime.

33 In the Spree Forest Biosphere Reserve

The Forest with a Hundred Waterways

The road ends, leaving only water: back to nature is the only option. Here in the Spree Forest, the dark gleaning water winds its way through deep forests, past fields and organic farms. The long flat punts (known as "Kaupen") are pushed, not rowed, through the watery labyrinth – it's the only way to travel through the 200 navigable (of about 300) canals and an experience unique to the Spree Forest. Cyclists, hikers and canoeists are also welcome. The fitting midday snack? The Spree Forest gherkin, considered by many the best of its kind, and potatoes served with quark and linseed oil. Around 18,000 different species of flora and fauna live in the biosphere reserve. A wide variety of accommodation is available, but most popular and typical is the wood cabin. Those in search of greater comfort should try Lübbenau Castle.
Tel.: +49 (0)354/2873-0, fax: 2873-666, www.schloss-luebbenau.de)

34 The Wurzburg Residence

Where Apollo greets the Prince-Bishop

Proof, of the universal admiration accorded to the largest Baroque construction in southern Germany was its inclusion, in 1981, on the register of UNESCO World Heritage Sites.
Balthasar Neumann built a vast and splendid stairwell for his Prince Bishop Schönborn, crowned with 600 square feet of frescoed ceilings: would it hold up in the complete absence of any supports? Almost 200 years later, Wurzburg did crumble under Allied attack, but the stairwell ceiling survived. A U.S. Army officer made sure that it was protected, fully aware that it housed one of the world's most splendid frescoes. Painted in 1752/53 by Giovanni Battista Tiepolo, it showed Apollo, God of the Arts, rendering homage to the Prince Bishop, watched by the four continents.
Today's visitors can admire the splendour of the Imperial Chamber, the White Chamber, the Garden Chamber and the Court Church, catching their reflections in the Rococo Hall of Mirrors and maybe relaxing in the garden.
HOTEL RECOMMENDATION: Zur Stadt Mainz, Semmelstr. 39, 97070 Würzburg, tel.: +49 (0)931/53155, fax: 58510, www.hotel-stadtmainz.de

Above: Balthasar Neumann's Baroque Residence, built for the Prince Bishop, is full of works of art and masterly architectural elements.

35 Sesslach – Where Small is Beautiful

The village of the beautiful half-timbered houses

This little town is neither as famous nor as rich as Rothenburg and only has one tenth of that city's population. Yet Sesslach, with its fortified city walls, is not dissimilar in atmosphere. It only takes a few minutes to walk through the town from one city gate to another – unless one stops to admire the alleys and gabled houses.
Sesslach, a former fore-rectory of Wurzburg, nestles amid hills and woods, which have shaped the tranquil old town around the Renaissance Magistrates' Court and several old inns. A poet spent his early years here: Friedrich Rückert (1788–1866), also known for his translations of Eastern and Middle Eastern poetry. Where might one find Sesslach? To the north of Bamberg, quite close to Coburg.
TOURIST-INFORMATION SESSLACH
Marktplatz 98, 96145 Sesslach,
tel.: +49 (0)9569-9225-40,
www.sesslach.de

The carefully restored old houses give this little town a friendly atmosphere.

The Bavarian Alps are Germany's most popular holiday destination: mountains and lakes stretching from the Chiemgau region to the Pfaffenwinkel and on to the Allgäu. The area is rich in natural beauty and cultural history – traces of which, such as King Ludwig II's quaint Schachenschloss (Schachen Castle) remain to fascinate modern-day visitors.

Germany's South

Centre of Breisgau's capital: the market with Minster and many charming architectural details, such as the Gothic oriel under colourful brickwork or the clock on the Minster spire. Opposite: The flower market by the Minster looks even better from on high. Freiburg has its quiet corners too, such as this one in Gerberau.

36 Freiburg – the Beauty of Breisgau

A pleasant place to do business: the market by the Minster

Local legend has it that a rich farmer from the Breisgau region was so enamoured of Freiburg's beautiful gates and spires, of its crooked alleys and the cosy alehouses that one day, he expressed the wish to load the whole thing up and take it home with him. Many a visitor will share his feelings.

Freiburg is smarter now that it was then, but the weekly market on the square by the Minster (cathedral) remains a fixture. Nowadays, there are many organic-food booths, but the little canalized streams still run alongside the pavements, fed with water from the Black Forest that is as clear as ever it was, and the inns still serve a wide selection of good wines. Those born and bred here tend to stay for ever – and because the town cannot be carried off, lock, stock and barrel, more and more visitors find themselves thinking about settling down here, especially at retirement age. This trend began in the last quarter of the 19th century, when Freiburg's imaginative Lord Mayor Otto Winterer (1846–1915) correctly assessed the town's natural advantages and decided to invest in tourism, attracting guests from northern Germany rather than industrial manufacturing.
Freiburg is considered the heart of the Breisgau and Southern Baden regions. It was fairly heavily bombarded during the war but today's visitors will see only picture-perfect restoration work: picturesque gables and bay windows, slate roofs and domestic water reservoirs. During a bombing raid on November 27th 1944, almost the entire old town was laid to waste within twenty minutes, although it contained no arms factories linked to the German war effort. Thousands of people burned to death or suffocated. The spire on the Minster was hit but not destroyed. The local population interpreted its survival as a sign of hope. Thanks to the help provided by the neighbouring Swiss city of Basle, the holes in the Minster roof were also quickly patched.

The most beautiful spire

Jakob Burckhardt (1818–1897), the great Swiss art historian, once praised the delicate openwork on the spire of Freiburg's Gothic Minster as the "most beautiful tower in Christendom". The photographer Peter Cornell Richter went one better, calling it the most beautiful tower in the world: according to Richter, the building unites the knowl-

Breathtaking: the delicate spire of Freiburg's Minster, one of the costliest works of German Gothic architecture. For those with stamina: the artworks in the cathedral's interior, from the high altar to the lively stained-glass windows (right) take time. Take a break afterwards on the markets (opposite above).

edge and skill of many civilisations – oriental, Hellenistic and Western. Richter found that certain proportional correlations matched those of ancient philosophies such as the correspondences between music and numbers elaborated by the Greek mathematician Pythagoras (around 580–496 BCE), and those between sounds and planetary motion (spherical harmonics) set out by the Greek philosopher Plato (427–347 BCE). Richter concluded that "the Minster's outer form and its interior are tonal music chiselled in stone, which makes the Minster a living body of stone harmonizing with light and sound." (*Klingender Stein. Das Freiburger Münster*, with large-scale photos, Freiburg im Breisgau 1990).

The beauty of Freiburg's Minster is multi-faceted. The slender spire rises over the valley against the backdrop of the Black Forest hills, and at a safe distance from the many multi-storey buildings on the town's outskirts. The spire is visible from nearly all over town, with flashes of blue sky shining through the elaborate openwork, enhancing its silhouette. The sound of bells fills the air: they were last renewed in the year 1959, except for the Hosanna Bell and Small Silver Bell, which both date from the mid-13th century. The organ music issues forth triumphantly from thick red sandstone walls, through the narthex and out onto the market place where the market court convened in the Middle Ages. There is a bewildering array of biblical sculptures, each with a story to tell, adorning the exterior and interior stonemasonry, most notably the high altar ensemble created by Hans Baldung Grien (a pupil of Albrecht Dürer) between 1512–1516, and the stained glass windows, some of which are older still.

The town and its people spent four hundred years, from 1218 to 1620, building the Minster, from the reign of the Staufer Imperial Dynasty to the Thirty Years' War. Restoration work is an ongoing project. The most important dates are 1350, when the building master Heinrich Müller completed the 116 metre-high spire, and the year 1513, when the last section of the Parish Church of the Virgin Mary was consecrated. The church has only been a cathedral since 1827, when Freiburg took over from Constance as Bishopric.

Between the Black Forest and wine-growing country

After 1945, the people of Freiburg decided to implement re-construction of the city based on its historic layout and a faithful restoration of the old buildings as far as possible. A wealth of architectural Renaissance and Baroque forms characterizing the pre-war era was recreated in the old town, whilst the sober commercial and administrative buildings of the post-war years were kept at a distance.

Whilst other German towns dismantled historic façades, in line with architect Adolf Loos' 1908 proclamation that "all ornamentation is a crime", Freiburg made sure that its Gründerzeit ("Founding Era" – from roughly 1850–1873) and Art Nouveau villas were declared listed monuments. Residential areas such as the Wiehre district on the outskirts of the old town south of the River

Dreisam, with its tree-lined streets and superbly preserved houses, are picture-book examples of conservationism. Freiburg has proved that honouring tradition and exploiting modern technology are compatible. Instead of tearing down whole districts to create a "car-friendly" network of urban thoroughfares, the small town on the River Dreisam invested in local public transport. In 1984, it became the first German municipality to offer its citizens a low-tariff Green Environmental Card, for use on buses and local trains. In 1996, it banned even buses from passing through the pedestrian zone, leaving only cyclists on wheels – much to the regret of pedestrians. But the arrangement works very much in favour of another Freiburg specialty: the little stone mosaics made with colourful pebbles taken from the Rhine and set into the cobblestones of the town's streets and alleys.

Freiburg's reputation as Germany's ecological capital adds to the town's quality of life. Back in 1977, the demonstrations by local students and members of the Green Party against the construction of a nuclear power plant at Wyhl on the Upper Rhine led to the foundation of the independent Öko-Institut (Ecological Society), a registered society that quickly developed into an authority on all things environmental.

In the summer of 2005, the Öko-Institut moved into new premises, the Sonnenschiff (Sun Ship) House, the world's first service constructed on the basis of 'Plusenergy' with solar panels and comprehensive insulation techniques that require only one tenth of the energy normally used to heat a building of this size.

EXCELLENT CUISINE IN A COSY ATMOSPHERE

A room with a view onto the Minster and onto the hustle and bustle of market life from early morning to late at night – welcome to the Hotel Oberkirch's Weinstuben. Visitors to the guesthouse only have a few steps to the Minster Square. Stay inside and enjoy the Baden wines that the locals have been imbibing here for the last 250 years. Today, the regionally influenced cuisine is considered one of the best in Freiburg, and a tiled stove and wooden panelling make for a cosy atmosphere. In the summer months, guests can enjoy Doris Hunn und Gudrun Johner's hospitality on an open terrace on the square.

Hotel Oberkirch's Weinstuben
Münsterplatz 22, 79098 Freiburg
tel.: +49 (0)761/2026868, fax: 2026869
www.hotel-oberkirch.de
26 rooms, 3 suites

FOR MORE INFORMATION ON FREIBURG

Freiburg Wirtschaft Touristik und Messe
tel.: +49 (0)761/3881880, fax: 37003
websites: www.fwtm.freiburg.de, www.freiburg.de, www.dompfarrei-freiburg.de, www.museumspass.com

80% of the Old Town was damaged during the war. Since then it has risen from the ashes. The fishing district (above) is particularly popular with visitors. The Town Hall richly decorated with sculpture and painting (below). Opposite: The Minster gargoyles, life on the market square; and the spire.

37 The People of Ulm, the Sparrows, and Einstein

The world's highest church tower

Travellers on the train from Stuttgart to Munich are in for a treat as they pass by Ulm: a stunning sequence of views of the tower of the Minster. Why not stop and take the time to look around this old town on the Danube, birthplace of Albert Einstein and site, more recently, of innovative contemporary architecture?

You'll have to crane your neck to get a full view of the spire, which rises an astonishing 161.53 metres from the market square. Looking down is easier, of course, once you've taken the 768 steps up to the observation platform, situated at a height of 143 metres. On clear days, the view stretches to the distant Alps and the main body of the cathedral with its five naves looks quite diminutive down below. Once inside, however, visitors to the Minster of Ulm will find the lofty, 42-metre-high vaulting in the main nave an awe-inspiring sight: an effect fully intended by Gothic era architects. There's more, of course: the hundreds of stained glass windows could fill a book all by themselves, with their unique range of biblical iconography and detail. Visitors do well to take a pair of binoculars along for closer study. Some salient dates: for one-and-a-half centuries, from 1377 to 1529, exceptional master builders such as the Parler Brothers, Ulrich von Ensingen, his son Matthias and Matthäus Böblinger were in charge of construction. Several times, the edifice was on the point of collapse. What an effort for a local parish church! In 1530, the majority of the citizens (87 percent) converted to Lutheranism, and the Minster followed suit, becoming a Protestant church. Building stopped, however, only to be resumed in the 19th century when general enthusiasm for all things Gothic led to the foundation of a new cathedral workshop in 1844. The spire was finally completed between 1885 and 1890 based on the daring plans of Matthäus Böblinger, rising to a height that just topped the Cathedral of Cologne (completed in 1880).

Ulm lost about 80 percent of its old town during World War II. But its citizens were determined to restore parts of the city and reconstructed what they could of their historic heritage. As a result, the cathedral is not situated, like its counterpart in Cologne, in the midst

Above: at a height of ca. 162 metres Minster only achieved its status as highest spire in the world in the late 19th century. Below: Profusion of frescoes on the Town Hall façade created by Martin Schaffner around 1540. Right: The Metzgerturm (Butcher's tower) of Ulm. Opposite: Ulm and the Danube. Opposite above: In the fishing district.

of modern metropolitan architecture but towers instead (at least on its northern side) over a network of smaller streets and alleys from the Wengengasse to the Hafengasse, from the Büchsengasse to Paradiesgasse. Most of these retain their original cobblestones. Some are now pedestrian zones with cafés and boutiques, jewellery and fashion stores.
The same applies to the fishing district, through which the River Blau flows to the Danube. The fishing district features half-timbered structures, old bridges and splendid old trees. Not far away, on the banks of the Danube itself, visitors can appreciate the charms and traditional beauty of a fortified imperial city, where the Butcher's Tower rises to dominate the steep gables layered beneath. The Town Hall is especially rich in painted ornamentation, with a richly illustrated late Gothic façade. The external chancel on the first floor testifies to the town's early confidence, around 1400, when citizens were subordinate to none but the Emperor himself. His imperial bailiff was forced to divest more and more of imperial powers to the local administration and as from 1473, the people of Ulm no longer honoured their ruler at the local Imperial stronghold of Weinhof, but in front of their own Town Hall.
Such hard-won rights are also celebrated on other occasions such as "Schwörmontag" (Oath Monday) in July, when a colourful procession of boats in all shapes and sizes proceeds down river in memory of the municipal constitution founded 600 years ago by guilds and patricians and sealed by the "Grand Oath".

"The sparrows know ..."

Many visitors to Ulm are astonished to see such a preponderance of unusually large sparrows dotted around the town – made from bronze, stone or artificial stone. In the year 2001, the town commissioned 250 "large sparrows" as a way of attracting money from sponsors for restoration work on the dilapidated southern tower of the Minster.
The sparrows have a story to tell: a legend, really, according to which early cathedral builders tried time and time again to load a beam horizontally on a cart and drive it through a narrow gate: it took a sparrow building its nest to show them that it is easier to push a straw through a narrow opening narrow end first. Without the sparrow "they'd be standing still before the gate/ their cart still stuck with all its weight/Maybe the sparrow's intuition/saved the spire from demolition."
The city's more recent buildings have risen more easily. The most spectacular

of these is situated right opposite the Minster, on a site originally occupied by a medieval monastery built by barefoot Franciscan monks before construction work on the Minster began. When the Minster became a Protestant church, the monks were forced to leave and their convent was demolished. Architectural contests were held, and prize-winning suggestions considered, but it was only at the end of the 20th century that the world-famous architect, the New Yorker Richard Meier, began work on Ulm's new Town Hall. Here as elsewhere, Meier worked with his typical combination of round and cubic forms, generous use of glass and a uniformly white façade. The result is a magnificent specimen of modern architecture in the spirit of Bauhaus design. The city's medieval tradition of employing only the best architects is evident elsewhere: the Neue Strasse, where some of the worst post-war building sins were perpetrated, has been chosen as the site for a series of large cultural and commercial buildings, including an "exclusive department store." Its architect is Stephan Braunfels, responsible for the Pinacothek der Moderne in Munich.

The city's most famous son remains unforgotten, even if he cannot actually be counted a citizen because his parents left the city before his first birthday: Albert Einstein. Visitors will find him immortalized above all in plaques and sculptures. In 1982, the Swiss founder of Ulm's "University of Design", Max Bill, had an abstract sculpture set up in Bahnhofstrasse, where Einstein was born; Jürgen Goertz' design for a fountain shows the scientist in iconic pose: sticking out his tongue; Calcutta's distant "Art Society" chose a spot next to Bill's sculpture for a plaque showing a likeness of Einstein's face. A stroll along the historic city walls by the Danube will take you past the latest addition to this collection: the Einstein sparrow at Adlerbastei 3.

COMFORT BEHIND A HISTORIC FAÇADE

The Schiefe Haus (Crooked House) is at least five hundred years old. It was renovated just ten years ago from the cellar to the attic when it opened its doors to hotel guests with just 11 well-appointed rooms tucked away behind the half-timbered façade. It is perfectly situated in the old town's fishing district, just a few minutes walk from the Minster, the Town Hall, and several museums.

Hotel Schiefes Haus
Schwörhausgasse 6, 89063 Ulm
tel.: +49 (0)731/96793-0, fax: 96793-33,
www.hotelschiefeshausulm@de

FOR MORE INFORMATION ON ULM

Tourist-Information der Ulm/Neu-Ulm Touristic GmbH
tel.: +49 (0)731/1612830, fax: 1611641
E-Mail info@tourismus.ulm.de
websites: www.tourismus.ulm.de,
www.muenster-ulm.de,
www.museum.ulm.de

38 Regensburg – The First Capital

From the Agilolfinger Dynasty to World Heritage City

Time-travellers exploring Regensburg's history should start at the Neupfarrplatz in the town centre, between two pedestrian zones, where two thousand years of urban history come together on one unique spot. Just a few steps down, six metres under the Neupfarrplatz, visitors will find the remains of a Roman legionnaire's camp. The journey can begin.

Local perspectives: cathedral towers rising over the Danube with the ancient stone bridge (left). Rooftop jumble – the view from St. Giles Church. Germany's oldest manufacturer of "Bratwurst", inside and out, at home in the Thundorferstrasse for 850 years now, and once again, a view down onto the slow waters of the Danube.

Only a small part of the camp has actually been uncovered. A more ambitious excavation would have involved digging up large areas of Regensburg's town centre. The remnants of walls and a tiled floor suggest the remains of a house, probably of a high-ranking officer, right on the Via Principalis – or Main Street – of the Castra Regina, the camp on the River Regen. Emperor Marcus Aurelius had the camp built in the year 179, the name stayed after the soldiers had left, was Germanised and used to refer to subsequent settlement. Regensburg is the place where the River Regen, flowing from its source in the Bohemian Forest, joins the River Danube.

The first dynasty of rulers, the Bavarian Agilolfinger, left no architectural traces at the Neupfarrplatz. Evidence of their reign can be found in the Jewish Quarter, first mentioned in records dated ca. 1000 – making it the second oldest in Germany (after Worms). The quarter comprises about 39 houses, including a Gothic synagogue and its Romanesque predecessor. The records also show that the quarter was self-administrating and employed Jewish judges. After five hundred years of local history, the district was dissolved and the Jews forced into exile following the death of their last protector, Hapsburg Emperor Maximilian in 1519. A pilgrimage chapel was erected on the spot where the synagogue once stood. It later became the first protestant church of the newly Protestant imperial city.

Comprehensive excavation work between 1995-98 unearthed the most spectacular treasure yet: 624 gold coins from the late 14th century. Equally spectacular and not to be missed, the document Neupfarrplatz – a multimedia show presenting a history of the Neupfarrplatzes, brilliantly combining contemporary technology and local history. For hundreds of years now, the Neupfarrplatz has attracted not only mercantile establishments but also political events and demonstrations. In 1919, the short-

HISTORISCHE
Wurstküche

A stroll through the old town to the Cathedral passes atmospheric spots such as (above) Haid Square, the Kepler House and Ducal Palace. Opposite: Building on St. Peter's Cathedral began in the 12th century, the towers were only completed in the 19th. Above right, columns on Walhalla, founded by the Bavarian King Ludwig I.

lived Republic of Soviets was proclaimed here. It was here that Hitler's supporters organized the public burning of books. And in 1942/43, a group opposing the National Socialist regime met here.

Restoring the Old Town: a delicate operation

The map of Bavaria shows a large triangle of three cities dominating the centre of the largest German Federal state: Munich on the River Isar, Nuremberg on the River Pegnitz and Regensburg on the Danube, the three capitals of Bavaria itself and of two subordinate regions, Franconia and the Upper Palatinate.

Of the three, Regensburg is the smallest but more than one thousand years older than the other two. The town was not as badly bombed during the war – all factors which combine to make Regensburg a city with real medieval flair, one of the most architecturally and structurally authentic not only in Bavaria but also in Germany.

A guided tour of the city comprises the old Town Hall, two historic salt barns, the stone bridge and gate, the Roman Porta Praetoria, the Cathedral and several other churches, elegant town houses, the Golden Tower and at least a dozen other items – including perhaps the Kepler House, dedicated to the memory of the great astronomer who died prematurely in Regensburg.

In addition to all its other attractions, Regensburg has succeeded in emulating the Austrian and Italian flair for restoring an old town district without losing its original charms. The old town in Regensburg happily merges modernity and tradition: book shops in Roman cellars, a hotel in a former Bishop's Palace, and a private Golf Museum run by an antique dealer in a carefully restored town house.

Treasure of Gold, Bridge of Stone

One of the city's focal points for over 250 years now has been its function as the seat of the princely Thurn und Taxis family, formerly successful postmasters to the Imperial Highnesses. The family originally hails from Lombardy and began organising imperial postal services in the 15th century, when it was still based in Frankfurt. In 1615, it rose to greater heights as Postmasters General of the Empire, a position held in perpetuity. The Thurn and Taxis family has resided in Regensburg since 1748, an obvious choice since the town was also home to the permanent Imperial Diet until 1806. It was only in 1867 that the German States secured the post monopoly – in return for some considerable compensation. The Thurn and Taxis Palace in Regensburg emerged from buildings that once constituted an Imperial Abbey.

St. Emmeram is an opulent Baroque palace – and now a museum – with lavishly appointed salons (the cloisters are the only feature of note to have survived from the building's ecclesiastical era). The treasures accumulated over the centuries by the Thurn and Taxis family were purchased from Princess Gloria by the Bavarian state, allowing them to remain in their original location, where they are still on view today in the palace's Princely Treasury, easily accessible to locals and guests alike.

Regensburg is rich in many respects: rich in charming urban panoramas, rich in European history, rich in churches, in its cathedral and in the patrician houses once built by medieval millionaires.
Yet what the locals appreciate most of all is an old Stone Bridge, the "old lady" spanning the Danube for nearly 860 years now: around the time of her construction, she was considered something of a world wonder. The Romanesque arch bridge has been built of natural stone and lime mortar, and heavily fortified for defense as well as durability.

However, the old bridge has began to crumble over the years. So by June 2005, a structure of braced steel beams was built to support the bridge. In 2007, the Stone Bridge was nominated for the award "Historic Landmark of Structural Engineering" in Germany. Since 2008 all vehicular traffic is banned from using the bridge. A new bridge for traffic is still under discussion, but that could be expensive: if the town is not to forfeit its World Heritage status, any new bridge must not be allowed to spoil the view of the old town down by the Danube.

PROSPERITY AND COMFORT

Formerly a residence of the Regensburg Bishops and situated close to the wonderful Cathedral of St. Peter, the Hotel Bischofshof has been home to prosperity and comfort for decades.

Hotel Bischofshof
Krauterer Markt 3, 93047 Regensburg
tel.: +49 (0)941/58460, fax: 5846146
www.hotel-bischofshof.de

FOR MORE INFORMATION ON REGENSBURG

Fremdenverkehrsamt im Alten Rathaus (tourist office in the Town Hall)
tel.: +49 (0)941/5074410, fax: 5074419
websites: www.regensburg.de/tourismus, www.regensburg.de/museumsportal

39 Meersburg – Treasure on Lake Constance

Vines, poetry and an old castle

One of Germany's foremost Romantic poets, Eduard Mörike, wrote of Lake Constance that it "calls out to us from afar". Rising from its shores, at an altitude of 480 metres above sea level, are Germany's highest vineyards. Elsewhere, this might present a problem. Here the lake's function as a heat reservoir more than compensates. The water surface serves as a huge mirror, reflecting the sun so efficiently that the vines can continue to absorb the warmth until late in the autumn.

Vines and flowers, palm trees and parks – it's all part of an overall picture guaranteed to please locals and visitors alike, who come here, to the shores of a lake bordering three countries, to enjoy the mild microclimate. Constance, Überlingen, Langenargen, Lindau: these are beautiful towns on Lake Constance, but many consider the former Bishop's palace of Meersburg as the real jewel in this crown. Situated opposite Constance on a hill above the lake, it sits amidst vineyards, resplendent in the glory of the "New Castle", commissioned by bishops in the mid-18th century and built by Balthasar Neumann (1687–1753), star architect and prolific master builder of the Baroque era, famous for the residence he built in Würzburg for the Prince Bishops. Meersburg's Old Castle is even more fascinating, with its distinctive step gable and rich historic inventory. The castle's origins lie in the mists of time, in the 7th or 8th century or even earlier, in the era of the Merovingian dynasty. It is considered the oldest inhabited castle in Germany. For a long time, it formed part of the vast estates belonging to the Prince Bishops of Würzburg, but has been privately owned for the last 150 years. The first of these owners was the renowned antiquary Baron von Lassberg, brother-in-law to the famous German poetess Annette von Droste-Hülshoff (1797–1848). Originally from the area around Münster, Droste-Hülshoff chose to settle here for the last decade of her life, recorded in passionate verse: "On the tower high I stand / ... reading maenad-like the storm/ wild wind in my hair". It was here that she fell in love with a younger man and succeeded in purchasing a small property, the

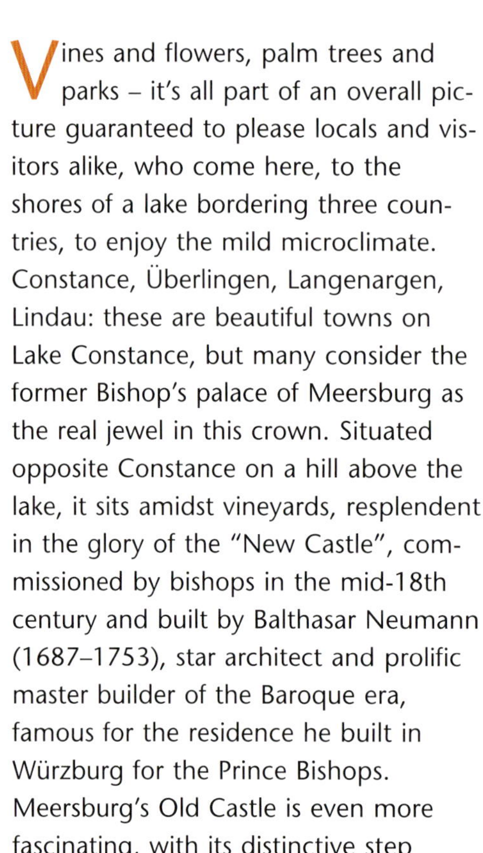

Centre: Home for over one thousand years to the Prince Bishops of Constance: Meersburg's New Castle, built according to plans drawn up by Balthasar Neumann from 1740–50. Below: wines from Lake Constance are much appreciated! Opposite: A town built for its citizens in which every house merits closer study.

"Prince's Cottage" located above the old town, where visitors can see her rooms furnished in the contemporary style. A couple of rooms in the castle itself are also dedicated to her memory and her visits to her sister and brother-in-law.

So Meersburg has much to offer, combining the charms and interests of a museum, the long distant past of medieval history and literary passion in the New Castle, Old Castle and Prince's Cabin respectively. These historic spots sit snugly in a small-town environment, uniquely rich in quaint alleys, squares and niches. There is constant movement between the upper and lower towns: pedestrians stroll up and down the Steigstrasse past colourful shops to the fortified gate – with more step gables – studying the half-timbered structures, ornamental wrought iron and painted shutters. There is plenty to enjoy down on the lakeside: walks in the shade of ancient plane trees or some respite in a cosy inn with panelled walls and heavy wooden tables such as the "Löwen" (Lion) and "Bär" (Bear) inns, painted in a warm red on which the bright green of the vines climbing up the façades stands out.

It might seem odd, at first glance, that the nostalgic surroundings of the New Castle should house a museum dedicated to the pioneer of aircraft manufacture. Friedrichshafen on Lake Constance was the site chosen by Count Zeppelin to carry out research and development work on his airship, and Claudius Dornier from the town of Kempten in the Allgäu region was one of Zeppelin's assistants, founding his own aircraft manufacturing company in Friedrichshafen in 1914.

COMFORT AND COSINESS FOR OVER 500 YEARS

The old bishopric has a Michelin-recommended romantic hotel, but why not chose the Löwen inn to overnight, which has welcomed guests here for over 500 years and has just completed a renovation and general enhancement of its simply appointed 21 rooms? The restaurant (closed from November to April) is located in a panelled room. Terrace also available.

Hotel Löwen

Marktplatz 2, 88709 Meersburg
tel.: +49 (0)7531/43040, fax: 430410
info@hotel-loewen-meersburg.de

FOR MORE INFORMATION ON MEERSBURG

Meersburg Tourismus

tel.: +49 (0)7532/440400, fax: 4404040
websites: www.meersburg.de, www.burg-meersburg.de

40 Bavarian Lake Constance: Lindau

Peninsula under a lucky star

The landscape around Lake Constance is enchanting. The lakeside shoreline around its gently lapping waves covers 263 kilometres (equalling the distance between Munich and Karlsruhe), whilst the mild climate favours the growth of palms, even banana trees. Throughout summer, the gardens blaze with hollyhocks, roses and delphiniums. Spectacular views of the lake and northern Alps open up around every corner, but the best view of all is onto the town of Lindau, formerly an island but now joined to the mainland both by road and rail. The connection is only 150 metres long, the railway dam about 500 metres wide. The area of water between the two, although part of Lake Constance, has its own, more modest designation: "The Little Lake".

Views of Lindau from the lake: the medieval Mangturm welcomes guests at the harbour whilst the Bavarian lion makes sure that Munich's rule is maintained. Opposite: it's a tight fit for the exclusive yachts down in the harbour and more fun out on the water in the sun and wind, far from the elegant villas and local villages.

Lindau is surrounded by a charming hilly landscape, by orchards and meadows and small farming communities through which visitors pass when coming into town. The western approach along the lake passes the little town of Wasserburg, coming from the east one passes the Allgäu Alps and from the north through Swabia and the towns of Leutkirch und Wangen. The main road leading to Friedrichshafen was rerouted inland years ago; the lakeside route is more modest and cannot take much traffic. It's only the southern approach from Bregenz that is dominated by large arterial roads, stretches of motorway and industrial sites. So come to Lindau by boat, like the traders crossing Lake Constance who made the town rich and prosperous.

Lindau's inhabitants number around 30,000, and not all of them live on the peninsula. Some prefer the garden city on the mainland. The town's roots go back to the 9th century, when a convent for noblewomen was founded on the island. The island developed into a settlement with enviable growth and stability, so much so that the neighbouring mainland community of Aeschach was forced to cede its market rights to Lindau in 1180 – only thirty years after Munich was founded. During the 13th century, Lindau was accorded the privi-

leges of an Imperial City and soon became known as the "Venice of Swabia" – a minor overstatement perhaps, but one which locals liked to hear. Trade in wheat and salt remained profitable and it was only after the old empire came to an end, and with it, the royal and imperial privileges and freedoms, that Lindau was forced to submit, in 1805, to the rule of Munich's ruling family, the Wittelsbachs, later becoming part of the Free State of Bavaria. King Maximilian II, son of Ludwig I (an enthusiast of the German Middle Ages), was so taken with Lindau that many noblemen and merchants from Munich chose to settle here, building representative homes on the shores of Lake Constance.

A tour of the city: a charming duty

A walk though the town centre of Lindau is more or less obligatory: although not completely car-free, the streets are quiet, encouraging pedestrians to take their time walking around, studying the splendid step gables and painted façades. The most impressive of these are on the old Town Hall on Maximilian Street and the "Haus zum Cavazzen".

The latter is particularly rich in imagery and iconography and is considered the most beautiful old town house in the Lake Constance area. Others include the Inn known as Gasthaus zum Sünfzen, parts of which date back to the 14th century, Haus Erath and the Haus zur Brotlaube. With all the cafés, bistros, shops and boutiques – there's plenty to see and do. Nonetheless, the distances are short and before you know it, you'll be down by the water in front of the Bavarian lion keeping watch over the harbour entrance. Created by the sculptor Johann von Halbig, the lion has resided here for 150 years in the shadow of Lindau's 33 metre-high lighthouse, not far from the remnants of another, somewhat older tower, the medieval Mangturm.

It's worth setting time aside to see the churches whose differing styles reflect both the fortunes and history of the town. St. Stephen's on the market square was constructed during the Gothic era but given a complete overhaul in the 16th century and endowed with a Baroque ceiling. St. Mary's Church, closely linked to the above-mentioned convent, is a comparatively modern structure, built by Johann Caspar Bagnatos in the mid 18th-century after its predecessor burned down.

The island's perimeter path is still popular with visitors and locals. The Thieves' Tower (Malefizturm) on the Schrannenplatz and the Powder Tower on the western shore are reminders of harder times. Evenings are best spent on the harbour: when the air is still warm and the lights shine on gables and balconies – that's when Lindau really glows.

RUSTIC AND INEXPENSIVE

The Hotel Brugger located by the municipal park with 23 comfortably and rustically appointed rooms, a conservatory and courtyards, all at a reasonable price (closed between mid-November and the end of December).

Hotel Brugger

Bei der Heidenmauer 11, 88131 Lindau

tel.: +49 (0)8382/93410, fax: 4133

www.hotel-garni-brugger.de

FURTHER INFORMATION ON LINDAU, LAKE CONSTANCE

Prolindau Marketing GmbH & Co. KG

tel.: +49 (0)8382/260030,

fax: 08382/260026

websites: www.prolindau.de

41 The Königswinkel Area around Schwangau

Neuschwanstein and More

The Wittelsbach dynasty was famous for finding pleasant spots for castles and palaces. King Ludwig II went one better when he chose the rocky promontory above the Pöllat Gorge as the site for Neuschwanstein Castle – a place of stunning natural beauty which satisfied the regent's love of unspoilt nature and his theatrical temperament. Situated between the steep slopes of the Tegelberg and the flanks of the Mount Säuling, the location amply fulfils all three Rs: romantic, remote, regal – unalterable prerequisites for building Neuschwanstein in the style of a historic "German Knight's Castle".

Centre: View onto the Bishopric of Füssen, close by the Königswinkel region. Below: the little church of St. Koloman nestles below the royal castles. Opposite: a dramatic backdrop for a knight's castle built for a king: Ludwig II's Neuschwanstein.

The following generations inflicted a few changes: one million visitors a year require certain changes in infrastructure. But an alliance of various interest groups comprising nature conservationists, fans of Ludwig II and of the castle itself have made sure that the damage is minimal, restricting the number of new buildings, conserving the forest that stretches up to the village of Hohenschwangau and making sure that the road up to the castle remains resolutely closed to all traffic. If you don't want to walk, you'll have to pay for a horse-drawn carriage. The protective zone surrounding the world-famous dream castle extends into the Alpine foothills, comprises the road connecting Schongau and Füssen and the area around Lake Forggen near the village of Schwangau.

For years, controversy raged around the building of the Musical Theatre on the southern shores of Lake Forggen near the village of Brunnen. It was completed nonetheless and is considered an architectural success, opening in 1999 with the premiere of the musical "Ludwig II", specially written for the occasion by Stephan Barbarinos. Within six months, far more than 25,0000 guests had indulged their unbroken enthusiasm for this legendary Bavarian King. The lively musical dabbles in romanticism and surprise special effects. Following a brief financial downturn, a second, equally popular, Ludwig musical was staged by the theatre.

The stunning landscape of the Königswinkel region in the Allgäu district, where the Alps rise dramatically from the plain and the choice of souvenirs is endless. Opposite: the medieval castle of Hohenschwangau, restored by King Maximilian II – and the unique view over Lake Alp, Lake Schwan and the Allgäu Alps.

Happily, the stunning landscape around Lake Alp and the Pöllat Gorge is big enough to accommodate Ludwig's many fans. If you take the circular trail that leaves from the village of Hohenschwangau, passing Lake Alp and Castle Hohenschwangau, you'll soon find yourselves more or less alone in the forests on the lake's western shore, communing with nature, whilst the great majority of visitors descend in droves upon Neuschwanstein.

As a child and young man, the future King Ludwig II experienced nature most intensely when out on long walks with his Prussian mother Marie and his brother Otto in the area around Castle Hohenschwangau. One such outing three days before Ludwig's 12th birthday on August 22nd, 1857 took them to Mount Säuling, a local mountain that rises to a height of two thousand metres above Lake Alp. The logistic efforts involved were considerable, comprising an entourage that included Baroness Fugger, lady-in-waiting to the queen, two tutors, a mountain guide as well as the court cook, Hölzelmeier, and a horde of carriers. According to court records, the royal court spent three hours enjoying the panoramic view from the summit before descending carefully over steep mountain paths to the village of Pflach in the Lech valley.

Admirers of swans before "Lohengrin"

The Castle Hohenschwangau, known in those days as "Schwanstein", was purchased by Ludwig's father, King Maximilian II, and saved from ruin. Despite its neo-Gothic façade, the real substance and much of the interior of Castle Hohenschwangau is actually medieval. Maximilian II spent his childhood in the shadow of his own genial father, the antiquarian Ludwig I, who seems to have bequeathed his charisma directly to his youthful grandson, Ludwig II. But Maximilian had his fair share of romantic flair: the Swan Knight's Hall reflects his pre-occupation with swans, with its frescos, elaborate centrepieces and blue-gold vaulting. Along with the Lohengrin Legend, it set the course for Ludwig II own fascination with swans, long before Richard Wagner composed his opera.

As crown prince, Ludwig II was not content with Hohenschwangau and began making his own plans. Crowned King before he had turned 20, the young monarch journeyed to Thuringia to study Castle Wartburg, his architectural ideal, and to France, to Castle Pierrefonds near Paris, recently restored by the French architect and medievalist, Viollet-le-Duc. Ludwig chose a rocky outcrop above the Pöllat Gorge for his castle, necessitating the removal of ruins that remained from a smaller medieval castle before there was sufficient space to start work on Ludwig's vision: Neuschwanstein.

Ludwig's enthusiasm for his project was expressed with typical hyperbole: "The spot is unsurpassed in beauty, holy and remote, a temple worthy of our divine friend, sole arbiter of salvation and benediction." For this was the core of the young king's plan: to create a refuge for Richard Wagner – "with a wonderful view into the mountains of Tyrol." Ludwig paid the master's considerable debts and promoted his operas in

Munich – yet he had not been able to keep Wagner in Munich, where public outrage over the often extravagant and sometimes thankless guest – as well as the planned construction of the Wagner Opera House above the banks of the River Isar – was rampant. Ludwig himself often suffered from Wagner's highly developed egoism, publicly vouching for Wagner's honour whilst the composer was in the midst of an adulterous affair with Cosima von Bülow, whom Wagner later married.

A lonely king and 50 million visitors

Ludwig initially estimated that Neuschwanstein would take three years to build. In fact, 16 years passed before he was able to take up residence for the first time, in 1884.

Richard Wagner died in the previous year: the guest apartments located directly under the throne room and intended for the composer remained unfinished, their mighty iron beams left un-plastered, a symbol of Ludwig's growing isolation and loneliness. Since the early 21st century, these rooms have been used as a visitors' centre, with a café, a souvenir shop and a video screening room, welcoming the castle's 50,000,000th visitor in July 2005.

But these old stories of the "Fairy-Tale King" and his sorry demise should not overshadow a visit to the enchanting landscape between Mount Tegel and Mount Säuling, around Lake Alp and the Pöllat Valley. The largest nature reserve in the Alpine region extends eastwards from the "Königswinkel" – the Ammergau Alps district between Lech und Loisach. The town of Füssen is not far, burial place of St. Magnus, a simple Irish monk. The surrounding German Alps are of breathtaking beauty – as anybody who has even been to the area around Königswinkel will confirm.

SIMPLE ELEGANCE

For over one hundred years the Schlosshotel Lisl has welcomed guests in spacious rooms and premises complete with terrace. The exterior of this former castle was extensively restored in 2005; the hotel is close to both the town centre and the woods. The 35 rooms, some with a view onto the royal palaces, are simply and elegantly appointed. The "Wittelsbacher Salon" restaurant specializes in Bavarian, national and international cuisine – and a royal view.

Schlosshotel Lisl & Jägerhaus
Neuschwansteinstrasse 1–3,
87645 Hohenschwangau
tel.: +49 (0)8362/8870, fax: 81107
www.lisl.de

FOR MORE INFORMATION ON THE KÖNIGSWINKEL REGION

Tourist-Information Hohenschwangau or Schwangau
Tickets for the castles available in the ticket centre
Hohenschwangau (time-slots allocated for same-day visits)
tel.: +49 (0)8362/930830, fax: 9308320
Websites: www.hohenschwangau.de, www.schwangau.de, www.festspielhaus-neuschwanstein.de

42 The Pilgrimage Church of Wies (Wieskirche)

A jewel of Bavarian rococo

A pilgrimage church dedicated to "Our Scourged Saviour of the Meadow" must be something special and it is: the epitome of Bavarian piety and 18th-century religious art. Thousands of pilgrims still come here, to this wondrously elaborate Rococo building, in search of salvation from the miracle-working image of the scourged Christ – release from suffering and the fulfilment of prayers.

The distant Alps form a panoramic backdrop; the encircling hills have been around since the ice age: the "priests' corner" with its valleys, villages and summer meadows is a natural home to the pilgrim church of the "Scourged Saviour." Generations gather here to worship; even the children wear local costume (opposite).

The figure of Christ on the main altar is neither sweet nor friendly. Hand-carved by two Premonstratensian monks from the monastery of Steingaden in 1730, their work feels clumsy – almost crude – but powerful, nonetheless. Later generations might call it expressionist. The image of Christ was originally intended for the Good Friday Procession, but soon disappeared into the attic of a local innkeeper. A relative later took the wooden figure to a farm "in the meadow" for safekeeping. On June 14th 1738 (the year in which the Pope excommunicated enlightened Freemasons) observers noted tears flowing down Christ's face. Hundreds, then thousands of believers came to see the miracle. In 1740, the statue was placed in a simple field chapel. Five years later, the crowds had increased again and the architect Dominikus Zimmermann (1685–1766) from Wessobrunn was contracted by the abbot of the neighbouring monastery of Steingaden to build the Wieskirche. Dominikus' older brother Johann Baptist (1680–1758), one of the era's most highly regarded fresco-painters and stucco plasterers, designed the interior. As early as 1779, the priest in charge of the church wrote a little pamphlet entitled "The True Origin and Progress of the scourged Saviour of the Meadow", noting the veritable invasion of pilgrims: "Why write more about the grace that emanates from this place – when pilgrims from all over the world have come to witness it for themselves: from as far afield as St. Petersburg in Russia, from Gotenburg in Sweden, from Amsterdam in Holland, from Copenhagen in Denmark, from Christianenburg (=Oslo) in Norway, from Nîmes in France, and from Cadiz in Spain?" There are other Rococo churches in the area – in Hohenfurch, in Rottenbuch, Wessobrunn and in Wildsteig. In fact, the whole region was

once referred to as a "priests' corner". From today's perspective, that might sound derogatory and antiquated. Back then, however, people were happy to enjoy the protection of local abbots, each one of whom was a small king in his own realm. No wars were waged – and efforts concentrated instead on supporting the local economy and building splendid churches. There was still enough money around to take care of the local populace once the abbot's own needs had been met.

"Come in, we are open!"

Even in this land of plenty, the Meadow Church stands out as a place of exceptional and cheerful piety. To see it at its best, make an early start to arrive at the church at first light whilst the surrounding hills and farms still slumber and solitary trees stand out against the woods and mountains beyond. The wide, red-tiled roof of the Wieskirche, its white-washed walls and delicate tower summon visitors from afar. It stands more or less alone on the gently rolling slopes – only one large inn is situated somewhat further down the hill – as if it were part of nature itself. There are only a few visitors around at nine in the morning – no crowds yet in the light-filled interior created by the Zimmermann brothers, whose celestial blue cupola invokes heaven itself. The golden glow of the side altars is offset by white walls, the waves and arches of silver lamps complemented by wrought iron railings. About one million visitors come every year. To pray? There aren't many signs around here prohibiting this or that, and there is no entrance fee either. The motto is: "Come in, we are open." The faithful are grateful and leave votive messages to the saints, little pieces of paper with requests and words of thanks. The priest is happy to have such an international crowd of visitors and appreciates their interest. During services, a attendant at the back of the church guarantees a modicum of peace and quiet.

Considerable efforts on the part of the church, the parish and the state have been necessary over the years to maintain the building. In 1803, after the secularisation of monasteries, the building seemed destined for demolition, but the surrounding farmers saved it with petitions and personal sacrifice. In 1983, the Bishop of Augsburg, Joseph Stimpfle, campaigned successfully for the revival of the "Brotherhood of the scourged Saviour of the Meadow" but for years, the building was shaken by reverberations from low-flying military aircraft. Finally, the flight paths were changed and the costly repairs could be carried out. Over ten million Deutschmarks were spent on restoration measures, including uncovering the original wall-paintings. Today the church is listed as a UNESCO World Heritage Site.

WELLNESS AND NATURE

The local town of Rottenbuch is home to the Moosbeck-Alm, which offers wellness programmes in a tranquil, rural environment: it occupies a sunny spot with a swimming pool heated by solar energy, sauna, Jacuzzi, and conservatory. The König-Ludwig-Stube Restaurant provides sustenance; bike rental and tanning beds are also available!

Moosbeck-Alm – Hans Gruber
Moos 36, 82401 Rottenbuch
tel.: +49 (0)8867/91200, fax: 912020
www.moosbeck-alm.de

FOR FURTHER INFORMATION

Pfarramt (Rectory) Wieskirche
tel.: +49 (0)8862/93293-0, fax: 93293-10
Websites: www.pfaffenwinkel.com, www.rottenbuch.de

43 Munich's Favourite Garden

Over two centuries of the "English Garden":

Pleasure in the Pleasure Gardens. For park lovers, there were two groundbreaking events in the year 1789 – even if history has favoured one in particular: in July of that year, the Parisians stormed the Bastille and in August, the Bavarian Prince Elector Karl Theodor decreed the laying out of an English Garden in Munich. The Hofgarten (Court Garden) attached to Munich's Residence Palace had been opened to the public in 1780. Now the larger area of land used as hunting grounds by the princes for over a century was to be transformed into a park for people "of all classes." It was a simple gesture, involving neither revolution nor the guillotine. Yet the new gardens were symptomatic of the new relationship between the Bavarian people and their ruler.

Wide open spaces in the middle of the city: a great place to take one's constitutional at any time of the day, and one more reason to love Munich. Tourists and locals mingle at the Chinese Tower to enjoy their beer – the Monopteros (opposite) is an ideal meeting place.

The real creators of the English Gardens in Munich were an American and a talented landscape gardener from the state of Hesse: Benjamin Thompson from Massachusetts, who was later raised to the peerage and named Count of Rumford, (1753–1814), and Friedrich Ludwig Sckell (1750–1823), who had been taught and learned to admire landscape gardening in England.
Both were destined for brilliant careers. Thompson, a highly talented experimental physicist, politician and military expert, went on to become Undersecretary of State in London and Minister of War in Bavaria, where he was also known as a social reformer. One of the many military and social projects that Thompson persuaded the prince elector to endorse was the transformation, in 1785, of princely hunting grounds to the north of Munich. Thompson used the grounds to cultivate plants used in military and veterinary medicine, to set up model farms and not least, to grow (and popularise) the potato. When it came to laying out a public park to be known as "The English Garden" in 1789, Thompson was able to call upon the services of Sckell. Although still relatively young, the master landscape gardener had already gained experience transforming the Schönbusch near Aschaffenburg and the Schlosspark in Schwetzingen into English landscape gardens.

The Eisbach, a tributary of the River Isar, flows through the English Gardens to the Kleinhesseloher See. Rowing round the central island is a favourite pastime and afterwards, it's just a few steps to the beer gardens, either at the Chinese Tower (opposite, above) or right on the lakeshore. Centre: Pavilion in the neighbouring Court Gardens (Hofgarten).

The reformer Rumford, forever in search of new challenges, moved to England in 1798 and from there, to Paris. Following a brief intermezzo with the rulers of Baden, Sckell chose to remain loyal to Munich. In 1804, he was appointed Director of the Royal Gardens and charged with extending and completing the park area between the River Isar and the Schwabinger stream up to and including the Aumeister inn. These were important years for the English Garden: provisionally landscaped areas now took on permanent form. And the English Garden grew to cover the territory it still occupies today, making it one of the most extensive city parks worldwide – smaller than the Bois de Boulogne in Paris and Phoenix Park in Dublin, slightly larger than New York's Central Park. (The 1.3 million inhabitants of Munich have a lot more per capita space – about six times as much – than New York's 7.4 million).

Landscaped gardens and its beloved features

Older inhabitants of Munich have spent about half a century enjoying the summer green and winter white of the English Garden between Prinzregentenstrasse and Kleinhesseloher Lake, as well as the northern area of the park beyond the arterial road known as the Isarring. Most of them have grown to love, to feel almost at home between the streams, meadows and copses carefully arranged to feel as natural as possible. Even the students from the neighbouring Ludwig Maximilian University grow so familiar with the artfully grouped trees, running brooks and well-worn paths (totalling 78 km, of which 12 are bridle paths) that it only takes a few semesters before they consider the gardens an extension of their living space. Attempts to change the park's appearance and use have nearly always been quashed. A sad exception to this rule was Hitler's Haus der Kunst (House of Art) along with the post-war enthusiasm for major traffic arteries such as the multi-Lane Isarring, part of the ring road cutting through the park to the north of Kleinhesseloher See.

But these are exceptions. It's quite easy to leave behind Munich's dense urban scene, the sounds of heavy traffic fade away to be replaced with birdsong and the feeling of having travelled back in time to an older and more charming era. Most of the park buildings were constructed under the reign of the Wittelsbach dynasty before the invention of the car. It was King Ludwig I in 1836, who instructed his court architect Leo von Klenze to build one of the park's landmark constructions, the "Monopteros" round temple, placed on a hill which Carl August Sckell had landscaped with debris gathered from building work on Munich's Residenz Palace. The neoclassical Rumford House, opened as an officer's mess in 1791 close to the Chinese Tower, is even older. The Chinese Tower itself was the first major building to adorn the English Garden, constructed in 1789/90 in the heyday of Europe's fascination with China, and based on the significantly higher Great Pagoda in London's Kew Gardens. Following its destruction by fire bombs in 1944, the exotic wooden construction was rebuilt and has

retained its role as meeting point for thousands of park-goers who congregate here and settle down on the adjacent benches of Munich's second largest beer garden. The Chinese Tower is a local landmark, beloved by young and old for its colourful carousel, whose enchanting figures, lamps and decorations are the epitome of old-world nostalgia and have long been considered synonymous with the charm of the English Garden.

Eat, drink and enjoy the view

There are plenty of other opportunities to sit down and enjoy the view: the slightly more elegant Seehaus beside the Kleinhesseloher See, the Millihaus situated by the Veterinärstrasse park entrance, the cosy Aumeister inn located in the Hirschau, and many others. On certain days, the authentic Japanese Teahouse, constructed for the 1972 Munich Olympics, (close to the Haus der Kunst) invites participants to original Japanese tea ceremonies. Activities on the nearby Eisbach (Ice Stream) are less esoteric: swimmers and surfers delight in the strong, cold currents whilst topless sun-worshippers watch from the adjacent safety of the Schönfeld Meadows. During the 1960s, much media attention was lavished on the nude bathing in the English Garden – making them even more famous. Today's visitors may be more interested in free wireless Internet, provided both by the beer gardens close to the Chinese Tower and the Seehaus. And according to a recent survey carried out by the *Süddeutsche Zeitung*, the best lookout point with free access is the Monopteros in the English Gardens, with views of the Bavarian State Chancellery, the new Town Hall, the Residenz Palace and Theatiner Church – not to mention the couples basking on the green lawns below.

THREE MINUTES FROM THE ENGLISH GARDEN

It's just a few steps from the English Garden to the Hotel Biederstein.
Hotel Biederstein
Keferstraße 18, 80802 München
tel.: +49 (0)89/3899970, fax: 389997389
www.Hotel-Biederstein.de

FOR MORE INFORMATION ON MUNICH'S ENGLISH GARDEN

Fremdenverkehrsamt (tourist office) in Munich,
tel.: +49 (0)89/2330300, fax: 23330269
tourismusverband München-Oberbayern.de
tel.: +49 (0)89/8292180, fax: 82921828
Websites: www.muenchen-tourist.de, www.muenchen.de, www.munich-info.de, www.schloesser.bayern.de

44 Werdenfelser Land between the Staffelsee and the Zugspitze

Painted houses and violin makers

Bavaria has always been associated with the stony splendour of the Karwendel and Wetterstein mountains. In fact, it was only 200 years ago that the former earldom of Werdenfels acceded to what is now the Free State of Bavaria. Until 1803, the Bishops of Freising were lords of the "Golden Land". Nonetheless, the locals have always considered themselves Bavarians.

Mountain hikes, crystal clear lakes, cattle in the meadows, village churches and beer gardens, local traditions and ancient customs – all that is best in Upper Bavaria can be found in the Werdenfelser Land. Centre: Garmisch-Partenkirchen in winter white. Below: Lake Gerold
Opposite: Castle Elmau

Today, the borough of Garmisch-Partenkirchen lies within the borders of the former earldom. Besides the Wetterstein and Karwendel Mountains it also comprises part of the Ammergau Alps to the west of Garmisch as well as the Ester Mountains to the east. The trade routes leading from Italy to Munich date back to antiquity – passing through the Loisach Valley and Partenkirchen, the village of Mittenwald and the Isar Valley – so poverty amongst the local hillside farmers was not as pronounced here as elsewhere in the Alps. Prosperity has been a byword in the Werdenfelser Land since well before the advent of tourism.

Who understands the dialect?

The inhabitants of the Werdenfelser Land have always been considered somewhat special. Even today, the locals only have to break into their regional dialect to create confusion amongst tourists and other outsiders. The idiom is considered purely Alpine, lightly overlaid with the raspy infections of Tyrolean. Nonetheless, "Ga-Pa", as Garmisch-Partenkirchen is sometimes referred to, is now a highly popular resort – the most popular tourist destination in the German Alps. It was all made possible by the train connection to Munich, established in 1899. The 1936 Winter Olympics really put this newly created town (the villages of Garmisch and Partenkirchen had been merged against their will in 1935) on the map, since when it has worked hard to maintain its reputation as a modern tourist centre, with sporting facilities, an extensive cultural calendar and plenty of shopping opportunities. Some events are famous far beyond the town's confines, notably the annual Richard Strauss Festival. Strauss, the composer of masterpieces such as the "Rosenkavalier" and "Salome", lived in Garmisch-

Partenkirchen from 1908 to 1949 in his Art Nouveau villa at Zöppritzstrasse 42. Visitors who choose to stay in town just need to look out of their hotel windows to enjoy the many views of the Werdenfelser Land, the Wetterstein Mountains and Germany's highest peak, the Zugspitze. Like Mittenwald, "Ga-Pa" is popular as a base for excursions into Tyrol, and is an El Dorado for ramblers and lovers of mountain lakes, streams and gorges (Partnach Gorge and Höllental Gorge), of Alpine forests and the meadows that flower so profusely in late spring. Every season has something to offer: the clear, mild autumn air, the larches turning yellow between the dark green pines or sunlight on the snow topped crests in winter – there is always something to delight the eye.

Inspired by nature

Ramblers on the trail from Partenkirchen via Graseck and the Kranzberg may come through the village of Mittenwald, famous for its locally manufactured violins and prettily painted houses. The Werdenfelser Land is awash with culture. Castle Elmau, located in the forests around Partenkirchen and Mittenwald, has been considered an iconic spot for over a century (it recently suffered severe damage during a fire but is already being rebuilt). A little further up, high above the Rein Valley, King Ludwig II built Schachen Castle: from the outside it looks like a hunting lodge, but step inside and you will find yourself in an oriental refuge of wondrous splendour. Even this, however, pales in comparison to Linderhof Palace in the Graswang valley to the west of the old – established convent school of Ettal, housed in a Baroque Benedictine monastery. In creating Linderhof, the King sought to realise his nostalgic vision of life at the court of the French Sun King, with gilded figures on fountains, sweeping flights of stairs, richly ornamented facades, and even more sumptuous interiors. The palace grounds with their exotic buildings merge seamlessly with the Ammer Mountains.
A few years after the completion of Linderhof Palace, the area welcomed a new cultural phenomenon: a group of artists who called themselves the Blauer Reiter (Blue Rider) settled in Murnau on Lake Staffel and began to paint in vibrant, resonant colours – paintings of intense expression like those of the Fauves (The Wild Ones) in France. Even today, a wonderful selection of art by Wassily Kandinsky, Gabriele Münter and Alexej Javlensky can be seen in Murnau's Castle Museum high above the marketplace, and in Gabriele Münter's house, now also a museum.

SIMPLE BAVARIAN PLEASURES

Situated at the heart of old Partenkirchen, the family-owned Fraundorfer Hotel has been specialising in Bavarian comfort since 1857. Some of the 30 rooms in the old hotel and its new annex, the guesthouse Barbara, have handicapped facilities or cater specifically to families. The rooms are appointed in the Bavarian style or colour-schemed, with special attention to children's needs. In-house sauna and solarium. The kitchen specialises in excellent Bavarian cuisine, local dance performances and sing-a-longs create a special atmosphere.
Gasthof Fraundorfer
Ludwigstrasse 24,
82467 Garmisch-Partenkirchen
tel.: +49 (0)8821/927-0, fax: 927-99
www.gasthof-fraundorfer.de

FOR MORE INFORMATION

Werdenfelser Land
Kur- und Ferienland
Garmisch-Partenkirchen
tel.: +49 (0)8821/180484, fax: 180485
websites: www.garmisch-partenkirchen.de

45 The Bavarian Sea

The Chiemsee and its islands:

White summer clouds scud across the sky, their reflections caught in the Chiemsee itself and in the dozens of smaller lakes and ponds dotting the surrounding woods and meadows. Bavaria is rich in lakes: the designation Chiemgau refers to its largest lake and the region around it with its many smaller expanses of water. The Eggstätter Seenplatte (Eggstätter Lake Plateau), for example, situated nearby in the woods around the Chiemsee, notches up a total of about 17 lakes and ponds.

Centre: 84 square kilometres of water: the Chiemsee and its three islands – pictured here against the backdrop of the Kampenwand. Below: Façade of Herrenchiemsee Palace, an incomplete, uninhabited Bavarian Versailles, home today to the King Ludwig II Museum. Opposite: Sunrise.

The area is popular with sailors and surfers, swimmers and ramblers. If you've had enough of the water, try your hands – or feet – at mountaineering or hiking on the Kampenwand above Aschau, Hochgern and Hochfelln, or elsewhere in the foothills of the Alps that rise from the lake shore. On very clear winter days – or when the local Föhn wind blows – the view from Seeon (home to Seeon Abbey, a Benedictine monastery founded to the north of Chiemsee over one thousand years ago) stretches as far as the Watzmann and the Großglockner in the Hohen Tauern range.

Gravel under your feet

The landscape around the Chiemsee is both grandiose and placid. High winds can whip up a real storm on the "Bavarian See". In fog, it seems to disappear altogether. But when the sun shines, the 84 square kilometres of water gleam and sparkle in the light. Lakeside paths attract ramblers keen to explore the mossy countryside between Bernau and the market town of Prien, far from busy roads and the Munich–Salzburg motorway. Another popular area is located to the north of Übersee, where birds enjoy the protection of a local conservation area, dragonflies dart and glitter over the water, and yellow lilies lie resplendently in the sun. It's quietest on the eastern shore between Chieming and Arlaching opposite the most popular western lakeshore path connecting the three coves between Prien and Gstadt – part of the 60 kilometre circular path.

The region's top attractions are located on the two main islands of Herrenchiemsee and Frauenchiemsee: Herrenchiemsee Palace, built by Ludwig II, and the romantic Minster on Frauenchiemsee. But the area around the lake also has plenty to offer.

Above: Winter wonderland on the lakeshore near the village of Rimsting, to the north of Prien. Centre: Picture-book Chiemsee landscape: scattered fruit trees, cows and church spires.
Below: Flowers and vegetable gardens flourish on the Fraueninsel.
Opposite: Island-hopping by boat – the best way to experience the lake!

Enchanting hinterland

Foremost amongst these sites are an artist's house, the precious frescoes of the legend of St James' in Urschalling (about one hour's walk from Wildenwart), the 800 square hectares that make up the Kendlmühlfilz, and the ancient Roman artefacts and remains exhibited in various local museums. The Exter Artist's House in Feldwies is an old farmhouse that served for many years as the summer studio of the painter and academy professor Julius Exter (1863–1939) whose landscape paintings glow with the extravagant colours normally associated with the Fauves such as Matisse, Derain and Marquet. A relatively rare rendition of the life of St. James can be seen in a romantic little church in Urschalling; Wildenwart has a palace built by the Wittelsbach dynasty and although its splendid gates are closed to tourists and strangers, the adjacent inn provides Bavarian comforts. The Kendlmühlfilz is a highland moor near Grassau, an almost primeval landscape of mosses, grasses and birches covering 800 square hectares, a nature reserve since 1992. The whole Chiemgau region remains largely agricultural, with wooden houses snuggling under broad gables, and a vibrant local cultural scene, much appreciated by visitors and tourists. And then, of course, there's Herrenchiemsee Palace.

Is this Versailles?

Even first-time visitors arriving by boat on Herrenchiemsee are familiar with King Ludwig II and his Bavarian Versailles. They come expecting gilded mirrors, chandeliers and royal four-poster beds – all of which can be admired in full. Bear in mind, however, that the splendour in Herrenschiemsee feels distinctly cool: Ludwig Thoma, one of the most popular Bavarian writers of the time, complained of the "pale imitation of Versailles," maintaining that the "overloaded and arbitrary gaudiness" made him shiver.

Like so many critics of Ludwig II, Thoma was wrong to accuse the King of displaying arbitrary taste. The sovereign had actually bought the 240-hectare island in 1873, a full five years before construction began. His purchase was spurred in part by a petition submitted by a deputation of local citizens asking that the wonderful highland woods on the island be preserved rather than felled to satisfy the rapacious greed of Swabian timber merchants. Ludwig was obsessed with detail and spent hours studying specialist literature. He travelled to Versailles and was more open to the modern technology of his time than most of his royal cousins. His idealistically architectural visions deliberately went against the grain of current building fashions and in executing them, he insisted on the highest standards: standards and skills amongst Bavarian craftsman improved considerably.

Herrenchiemsee Palace is a strange mixture of Bavarian and Bourbon heritage: even the Hall of Mirrors is several metres longer than the original in Versailles. Tour guides dwell on details such as the dozens of women who worked on the royal bedspread for seven years. Ludwig himself intended to inhabit a very small part of the palace. Most of the rooms were laid out as a monument and

memorial to the much admired Sun King, Louis XIV. Herrenchiemsee Palace was never completed. The royal treasury was almost completely empty when Ludwig II came here for nine days and nights from 7th – 16th September 1885 – his first and last visit.
He once said that he would never open his castles and palaces to the public for fear that they would "desecrate these holy halls." In the end, this too remained but a fond hope and it must be said, in retrospect, that the legacy of his royal edifices benefited his country more than the many wars undertaken by Louis XIV, whose territorial conquests were not to outlive his reign. Many palace visitors remain unaware of the beautifully landscaped paths leading through the palace grounds, and not many know that an assembly of high-ranking lawyers gathered here at the old castle (a former monastery building) in 1948 to draw up Germany's post-war constitution (Basic Law). The island also has ruins of Celtic ramparts and an early Benedictine convent founded by an Irish monk in the 7th century, later transferred to the Augustinian Rule and secularised in 1803.
The much smaller island of Frauenchiemsee, the Fraueninsel or "Ladies' Island", is known for its gardens, many of which are replanted every year with new and fantastically colourful flowers. The island convent dates from the Carolingian era but is far more than just a museum. Benedictine nuns continue to live and work here. The sculptures and wall paintings adorning the premises are hundreds of years old: some even go back over 1000 years – vibrant links to an ancient past. This island of nuns, fishermen, gardeners and innkeepers is a gentle place, its 13.5 square hectares one of the most endearing spots in the entire Chiemsee region.

A CLEAR VIEW ONTO THE LAKE

The Hotel Wassermann, run by the Stocker family in Seebruck is ideal for a comfortable holiday in the Chiemsee area. Leisure activities include sailing and surfing courses, canoeing and kayaking, rafting on the Ache and Alz rivers, bike tours – and an indoor pool, and wellness spa.

Hotel Wassermann
Ludwig-Thoma-Strasse 1
83358 Seebruck am Chiemsee
tel.: +49 (0)8667/871-0, fax: 871-498
www.hotel-wassermann.de

FOR MORE INFORMATION

Chiemsee-Tourismus KG
tel.: +49 (0)861/965550, fax: 9655530
Schloss- und Gartenverwaltung Herrenchiemsee
tel. +49 (0)8051/6887-0, fax 688799
Chiemsee-Schifffahrt (boating) Ludwig Fessler
tel.: +49 (0)8051/6090,
fax: (0)8051/62943
websites: www.chiemseetourismus.de,
www.chiemsee.de, www.derchiemgauer.de
www.chiemsee.bayern-online.de

46 National Park Berchtesgaden

Wilderness around the Watzmann

Golden eagles are considered a special – and increasingly familiar – sight, but there are plenty of other birds and animals to see in the Berchtesgaden National Park: wood and black grouse, the black and the three-toed woodpecker or the Apollo butterfly. Park attendants tend not to mention the Skandal chamois and the alpine ibex, whose V-shaped horns have become quite a common sight again throughout the Alpine regions. Groundhogs are plentiful in the area around the Königssee, where they are known for their high-pitched whistle. Other species returning to the area after a long absence include the lynx and the bearded vulture. Chances are, you'll see an Alpine salamander, and be careful where you put your feet: vipers are quite common here, whereas bears haven't been seen for a long time – or have they?

Considered by many to be Germany's most beautiful lake: the Königssee, surrounded on all sides by rocks and mountains including the Watzmann Massif, reflected here in its waters – an imposing sight. Opposite: bringing down cattle from higher meadows before winter sets in is a traditional Bavarian event.

Encouraging wilderness" is the kind nature conservation practiced in the 210 square kilometres that make up the Berchtesgaden National Park, encompassing Germany's most magnificent Alpine region (first declared a nature conservation area in 1921). The park is committed to welcoming visitors and letting them just experience the wild. This cannot be achieved without compromise. To get into the park, visitors must pass through Schönau, part of the Königssee region. This is a compromise, but a good one. When the national park was founded in 1978, the two municipalities of Königssee and Schönau merged. The fields of Schönau actually border on Berchtesgaden, between Königssee and the River Ramsaue. The national park has brought prosperity to the town of Schönau and its 6,000 inhabitants, where up to 8,000 tourists and at least 4,000 cars can be accommodated.

The holiday season brings a huge influx of visitors and it can get a bit crowded down by the Königssee itself. Dozens of crowded little electric boats chug over Lake Königssee. The locals are proud of the lake's drinking water quality and don't appreciate littering. It doesn't take long before the boats arrive at the steep face of the Watzmann, the motors idling in the water whilst trumpets and bugles

Splendid views in all directions: onto the Reiteralpe, reflected here in the Hintersee, onto the little Baroque-capped church in the Ramsau area and, once again, onto the walls and summit of the Watzmann. Opposite: Augustinian monastery and salt works, summer breezes and winter sports: Berchtesgaden. Right: locals at work in the National Park.

are sounded to test the echo bouncing back from the rocks. It's an impressive show, and one for which visitors are happy to leave a very generous tip. Warm-hearted comfort and high drama are two sides of the coin in the Bavarian Alps. Seen from a purely geographical point of view, the Berchtesgaden National Park incorporates almost the entire Königssee as well as the region comprising the south-eastern extremities of Germany, including the alpine giant known as Watzmann as well as the Hochkalter massif and the northernmost Alpine glacier.

Around 1800: "With wonder, joy and fear"

Only experienced mountaineers should attempt to climb the Watzmann. If you're fit you should make it as far as the "Watzmannhaus" (Watzmann Hut) quite easily, but the climb up to the Mittelgipfel (Mid Peak at 2,713 metres) is something of a challenge requiring sure footing and a good head for heights.

The first officially recorded ascent was completed by a student of theology from Salzburg who was evidently fascinated by botany and surveying: Valentin Stanig – portrayed in old age with a high forehead and pronounced chin – first climbed to the Watzmann-Hocheck in 1799 or 1800, before carrying on alone over the narrow ridge to the Mittelspitze (Mid Peak):

"… for some of the time I edged along the sharp ridge in a sitting position, at other times I seemed almost to drift through the air, upwards over steep rock faces… it took all my strength to cross the scree and finally reach the highest point of the Watzmann. Back where I had left them, my comrades watched me with wonder, joy and fear as I made my way up to the summit in the clouds."

The western, southern and northern flanks of the national park border onto Austria. Three great valleys (Königssee, Klausbach Valley and Wimbach Valley) and the roaring streams that made them are the topologically defining elements of these mountains.

Up in the Alps and down by the lake

The view from up high down onto the Königssee must be one of the most beautiful in the Alps – which is saying something. The azure sky reflected far below in the deep blue waters of the lake – it looks like a jewel growing there naturally between imposing rock faces and cliffs. Visitors come back again and again to look and marvel. The lake was actually formed by a glacier advancing from the Steinernes Meer mountain, ploughing through the valley and pushing scree to the place now occupied by the Königssee, which formed when the glacial waters melted. About 10,000 years ago, the glacier reformed during a colder weather period, ultimately leaving behind a wall of moraine debris as well as the upper lake above the Saletalm hut.

It's only from high up that one really appreciates the size of the famous Königssee. The pilgrimage church of St. Bartholomä looks tiny by comparison, with its two helmet-capped towers (built 1670/72) delicately positioned on

the narrow spit of land under the Watzmann!
The princely provosts of Berchtesgaden retained control of the area until the early 19th century (when they were replaced by the Bavarian Kings) and used the promontory as a base for fishing and hunting. Their simple hunting lodge is located directly next to the church and has been a popular inn ever since 1919 after the abdication of the last Bavarian king, Ludwig III.
The pilgrims who come from Pinzgau in Austria via the Steinernes Meer on the feast-day of St Bartholomew (August 24th) have been around for longer than the Bavarian kings and have making the pilgrimage since at least 1699, as is evident from the date inscribed in the church. There are no rooms in which to spend the night and access to St. Bartholomä is cumbersome, possible only by a steep mountain path.

Hikers in the National Park are spoilt for choice with a network of paths totalling roughly 190 kilometres. Guided tours are available free of charge all year round and vary both in length and emphasis. A small fee is charged for special request tours for smaller groups (seven or more participants). The lakeside path to the Malerwinkel (Painter's Point) outlook is easy walking. Alternatively, take the cable car up to the Jenner Outlook.

VIEW ONTO THE MOUNTAINS

Situated on the edge of the woods in the little town of Schönau, the Hotel Georgenhof boasts a splendid view of the mountains and an "Ecological Awareness Award" as well as a Michelin "Bib" for its cost-benefit logo. Its large garden features plenty of recliners, the café restaurant and assembly rooms in the hotel itself have tiled ovens for the comforts of hotel guests, there is a conservatory with an open fire and last but not least a sauna, solariums, and massages. Busstop three minutes walk away. Five single and nine and double rooms, eight multi-bed rooms.

Georgenhof
Modereggweg 21, 83471 Oberschönau
tel.: +49 (0)8652/9500, fax: 950200

FOR MORE INFORMATION ON THE BERCHTESGADEN NATIONAL PARK

Berchtesgadener Land Tourismus GmbH
tel.: +49 (0)8652/967215,
fax: +49 (0)8652/967402
websites: www.berchtesgadener-land.com,
www.bayerische-seenschifffahrt.de

Above: Am Großen Arber (1,456 m) in the Bavarian Forest. Bears and wolves, wisents and wood grouse have returned.

47 Bavarian Forest National Park

Primeval forest in Germany

Signposts point the way through the thickets, some of it over boardwalks. A new, young forest is growing up all around out of dead wood and toppled trees, evident from the various saplings poking through the undergrowth. There are no signs of human intervention, just a forest returning to nature. The foresters plant no trees, there are no pesticides in use. This was Germany's first National Park, founded in 1970 and it did not take long for the dense undergrowth to overrun the granite rocks that form the local mountains. There were frequent protests when the bark beetle was allowed to prosper unchecked, wreaking significant damage on the local spruce monoculture.

It is astonishing to see how nature regenerates itself. Rare animals such as the black stork and wildcat have also returned. Outdoor enclosures with wolves and bears remind us of the fauna that originally roamed here.

HOTEL RECOMMENDATION close to the National Park:

Landhotel Tannenhof, am Waldrand. Auf der List 27, 94518 Spiegelau, tel.: +49 (0)8553/9730, fax: 973200, landhotel-tannenhof@t-online-de

Below: popular venue for events past and present: Munich's Olympic tent-roof stadium.

48 Munich's Second Fairground

Olympic heights

From today's point of view it appears nothing short of a miracle that despite all the controversy and discussion, the Stuttgart professor Frei Otto was actually allowed to build the 75,000 square metres of tent roofing covering the 1972 Olympic stadium, evidence of an architectural sense of adventure less pronounced now than 40 years ago. The construction process had to overcome several obstacles but once it was completed the unusual tent stadium generated widespread enthusiasm, proving that large-scale architecture could be light, airy and original. The people of Munich quickly adopted the meadows, hills and lakes surrounding the stadium. Known today as the Olympic Park, it is a popular venue for summer and winter festivals. It is certainly prettier to look at than the Theresienwiese on which the Oktoberfest is held. 25 years later, in 1998, the stadium was declared a protected monument.

HOTEL RECOMMENDATION: Cosmopolitan, Hohenzollernstr. 5, 80801 Munich, tel.: +49 (0)89/383810, fax: 38381111, cosmo@cosmopolitan-hotel.de

49 Mainau Island

Flower show on Lake Constance

The park wonderland of Mainau is linked to the mainland by a causeway and is also accessible by boat. The Rose Garden, the Baroque castle, greenhouses featuring palms and orchids, the Italian water cascade, works of art and seasonal highlights such as thousands of tulips on the southern slopes, concerts and exhibitions, wine tastings: visitors will find more than enough to see and do – including perhaps a meal in one of the island restaurants.
When Baron Lennart Bernadotte inherited the island Park in 1932, he found it completely overgrown. His love of nature and lively imagination helped him turn the island into a very special place. After his death, his wife, Sonja Bernadotte af Wisborg, continued to manage successfully the "Blumeninsel Mainau GmbH" foundation.
No provisions have been made for guests to overnight on the island! The city of Constance is not far away however, and visitors will feel welcome in the three-star Hotel Barbarossa, situated in the old town on Obermarkt 8–12, 78462 Konstanz am Bodensee, tel.: +49 (0)7531/128990, fax: 12899–700; www.barbarossa-hotel.com

about 450 staff maintain the sumptuous flora on Mainau Island, Germany's most visited garden show. In the foreground Bernadotte Castle.

50 Höri – the Quiet Peninsula

Poet's dream, Artist's refuge

"No one comes here to Gaienhofen, it's too far off the beaten track", wrote Hermann Hesse in 1904. The newly married author had rented a farmhouse on Höri peninsula, simple and very quiet. He spent some years in Gaienhofen, enjoying his cottage garden and the company of his family. His desk can be seen in the farmhouse.
The former schoolhouse next door is now the local Höri Museum. The view from Horn onto the peninsula of Mettnau and Reichenau island is one of stunning tranquillity. The lakeside villages of Öhningen or Gaienhofen are ideal points of departure for rambles through dense forests. The expressionist painter Otto Dix chose the remote village of Hemmenhofen as a place of refuge when he and his art were persecuted by the National Socialists. His house (Otto-Dix-Weg 6) is open to the public. The countryside described by Hesse in "Luft von Opal und Perlmutter" is home to the Guesthouse Verena, Kirchgasse 1, 78343 Gaienhofen-Horn, tel.: +49 (0)7735/93380, fax: 933859, hirschen-horn@t-online.de

The island of Höri: a place of quiet, unostentatious contentment.

Above: Summer days in Schleswig-Holstein are drenched in the scent of cottage garden flowers – such as those in Bosau, round the old thatched houses. Below: More flowers and more thatched cottages on the Baltic Coast, in the Dars region of Mecklenburg Western-Pomerania.

Index

Hamburg's historic warehouse district with its quiet canals will be part of the new Hafencity, an urban development designed to merge modern offices with old functional buildings, comfortable flats and new cultural institutions, making the port of Hamburg – one of Europe's top transhipment points – even more attractive.

Back in the park of Sanssouci Palace: statues of European and Asian derivation such as this neo-classical youth and a Chinese gentlewoman look out over trees and lawns, fountains and flowers envisaged as a kind of ideal landscape by King Frederick II.

Imprint

Product manager of the English Edition:
Dr. Birgit Kneip
Translation: Eve Lucas, Bruessel
Proofreading: Jane Michael, Munich
Layout: graphitecture, Rosenheim
Repro: Repro Ludwig, Zell am See
Jacket design: Anna Katavic supported by photos of Bildagentur laif (c., a., b.) and Bildagentur Huber (a.l.)
Cartography: Astrid Fischer-Leitl, Munich
Production: Bettina Schippel
Printed in Italy by Printer Trento

This work has been carefully researched by the author and kept up to date as well as checked by the publisher for coherence. However, the publishing house can assume no liability for the accuracy of the data contained herein.
We are always grateful for suggestions and advice. Please send your comments to:

Bruckmann Verlag, Editorial Department
Postfach 400209, 80702 München
E-mail: lektorat@bruckmann.de

Further captions:
Jacket, front: above: Lightfire on Sylt;
centre: Moselle near Cochel; below: view on the Zugspitze.
Jacket, backside: Stralsund, Geroldsee, Fraueninsel.
Endpaper: the Olympic Stadium in Munich (B. Römmelt);
page 1: Cupola of Berlin's Reichstag
page 2/3: Riegsee with the Zugspitze massif (B. Römmelt);
page164/165: Loisach with Herzogstand and Heimgarten (B. Römmelt).
Endpaper: Small islands in the Bodden landscape of the Upper Pomeranian National Park. (Bildagentur Look)

Credits:
B. Römmelt: 2,3, 10 a.c., 11, 12 c., 122-123, 144-145, 146 b., 150-151, 152a.., 153, 154, 155 c., 156, 157, 158, 159 c., M. Kolberg: 13, 14-15, 45, 166; O. Heinze: 16, 17; J. Hellmuth: 108-111, 135, 140, 143: Bild-agentur laif: 23 u. (Eisermann), 24 c. (Lengler), 27 a. (Modrow), 29 r. (Glücklich), 29 l. (Eisermann), 53 r.a. (Böning/Zenit), 53 b. (Galli), 57 a. (Zielske), 57 l. b. (Langrock/Zenit), 57 r.b. (Galli), 62/63 (Kohlbecher), 67 l.a. (Gaasterland), 67 l.a. (Gaasterland), 67 a. (Gaasterland),
68 a. (Gaasterland), 71 b. (Kreuels), 75 a. (Zielske), 75 b. (Böning/Zenit), 77 a. (Tast), 79 a. (Zielske), 79 l.b. (Barth), 79 r.b. (Barth), 83 o. (Zanettini), 83 b. (Babovic), 85 l.a. (Babovic), 85r.a. (Zanettini), 92 a. (Modrow), 93 l.a. (Zielske), 93r.a. (Kirchner), 95 (Zielske), 97 b. (Bialobrzeski), 105 (Zielske), 106 a. (Naegele), 106 c. (Naegele), 106 b. (Eid), 125 a. (Emmler), 125b. (Bungert), 132 b. (Selbach), 133 a. (Selbach), 133 l.b. and r.b. (Selbach), 142 c. (Sahm), 162/163 (Adenis/Gaff);
Reinhard Feldrapp: 113, 115 b
Bildagentur Huber: 23 a., (Edmaier), U. Böttcher: 18 r.b.; M. Neumann: 67 c.; picture alliance/dpa: S. 76 r. (bildagentur-online/Exß); 78 l.b., 80 l.a. (beide: Schutt), 88 l.a. (Dirscherl), 114 r. (bildagentur-online/Celeste), 117 r. (Gehrig), 117 a. (bildagentur-online/Begsteiger), 117 b. (bildagentur-online/Forkel), 130 a. (bildagentur-online/Forkel), 145 b.c. (4 x bildagentur-online/Celeste).
All others: Thomas Kliem.

Die Deutsche Nationalbibliothek verzeichnet diese Publikation in der Deutschen Nationalbibliografie; detaillierte bibliografische Daten sind im Internet über http://dnb-nb.de abrufbar.

ISBN 978-3-7654-5253-6